Adam's insights have so many parallels to the world of athletics. The book offers stories about the times we fall and grow, win, lose, and find motivation. It's got life lessons for every coach, athlete, business person, and human.

Jeremy Fischer
Director and Head Coach—USA Track and Field Residence Program Chula Vista and World Athletics Lead Instructor; Coached Athletes to 15 Olympic and World Championship Medals

I love the way Adam thinks and this book doesn't disappoint. Every chapter left me feeling smarter and more inspired. It's a must-read for anyone who wants to crush life.

Dan Richards
CEO, Global Rescue

This thought-provoking and motivating book made me analyze much of my own life and I believe it could be helpful for anyone because the lessons are all-encompassing and timeless.

Taylor Amann
All-American Pole Vaulter and American Ninja Warrior Finalist

WHAT DOES YOUR FORTUNE COOKIE SAY?

80 IMPORTANT LIFE LESSONS THE
UNIVERSE IS TRYING TO SHARE WITH YOU.

ADAM ALBRECHT

Copyright © 2021 by Ripples Media

All rights reserved. No part of this book may be reproduced or used in any manner without written permission of the copyright owner except for the use of quotations in a book review. For more information: contact@ripples.media

First printing 2021

Book design by Joe Kayse and Najdan Mancic

ISBN 979-8-9853234-1-2 Paperback
ISBN 979-8-9853234-2-9 Hardback
ISBN 979-8-9853234-0-5 Ebook

Published by Ripples Media
www.ripples.media

DEDICATION

To my children Ava, Johann, and Magnus.
I hope this helps.

TABLE OF CONTENTS

Introduction 1
A Note About Fortune Cookies 5

1. Constantly Upgrade Your Thinking. 9
2. The Best Way To Live A Great Life Is To Start At The End. 12
3. Take Advantage Of The Golden Opportunities That Come Your Way. .. 16
4. Say Yes And No With Great Purpose. 19
5. A Great Life Starts With A Great Plan. 21
6. The Person Who Collects The Most Moments Of Bliss Wins. 24
7. Discover Your Knowledge Chain And Keep Adding Links. 28
8. The Person With The Most Keys Will Open The Most Doors. 32
9. It's The First Step That Matters Most. 35
10. Get On Top Of Your Day Before Your Day Gets On Top Of You. 39
11. Disappointment Is The Most Powerful Motivator. 41
12. Never Give Up. 44
13. Pressure Makes You More. 48
14. Nothing Will Happen Unless You Make It So. 50
15. The Set Of Your Sails Determines The Way You Go. 53
16. Focus On What You Can Impact. 57
17. Kick Start Your Day With A Smile. 60
18. Put On A Smile Every Time You Dial. 62
19. Think Bigger. 64
20. Your Success Is Directly Related To Your Contribution. 67
21. Assume The Defining Event Of Your Life Is Yet To Come. 69
22. Fill Your Attitude With Helium. 71
23. You're Either Getting Better Or You're Getting Worse. 74
24. Course Corrections Keep Your Path True. 76
25. Always Know Where You Are On Your Journey. 79

26. Grow Toward The Ideal You Every Day. 83
27. Focus On What You Want The Most. 86
28. You Can Change Your Life In One Day. 89
29. Forget Everything That Doesn't Help You Win. 92
30. Do What You Do Not Know And You Will Learn. 94
31. Celebrate Your Attempts. 98
32. Start. And Improve From There. 101
33. The Path To Great Achievement Is Lined With Fake Deadlines. 104
34. Start Before The Start. 107
35. Early Mornings Beat Late Nights. 110
36. Ask For What You Want. 113
37. Why Not You? 117
38. Always Bet On Yourself. 122
39. Don't Build A Network. Build Friendships. 125
40. Invest In People When They Are down. 128
41. Become A Better Listener. 131
42. Put The Results In Their Hands. 135
43. Read To Learn. Then Act. 138
44. Arrive Smarter Than You Left. 141
45. Take Small Steps To Make Giant Leaps. 145
46. Start Slower To Go Farther. 148
47. Today's Success Was Born Yesterday. 152
48. Today Is A Whole Different Day. 155
49. Build Your Ark Under Blue Skies. 157
50. Your Critical Electives Matter Most. 160
51. Success Is Mapped Out Day By Day. 163
52. Bring Something Special To The Party If You Want To Be Invited Back. ...166
53. Dream It Up. Write It Down. Build It Out. 170
54. Let Envy Be Your Guide. 174
55. Resolve To Be Successful. 178

56. Make Up A Great Story, Then Make It Come True. 180
57. Do Something Unreasonable To Become Unforgettable. 183
58. Go To Bed 30 Minutes Early. 186
59. If You Can Learn To Double Dutch, You Can Learn Anything. 189
60. Imagine You're The Only One Who Can Solve The Problem. 193
61. Always Play The Host. 196
62. Do Small Things With Big Bangs. 200
63. Everything Changes When You Exchange Names. 203
64. Initiate, Connect, And Reconnect. 206
65. Lean On Others To Accomplish More. 210
66. Focus On Your Most Important Thing And Make It King. 214
67. Block Your Calendar To Put Time To Work For You. 217
68. Wasting Time Is Wasting Your Life. 220
69. Your Time On Task Determines Your Success. 223
70. Investments In Growth Pay Out The Most. 225
71. The Best Opportunities Come With Short Deadlines. 229
72. Fear Is A Yellow Light. Not A Stoplight. 232
73. Find Your Sliver Mentors. 235
74. Get Just A Bit Better Every Day. 238
75. Find Your Secret Language And Master It. 241
76. Establish Your Priorities Or Someone Else Will. 245
77. Don't Balance Work And Life. Integrate Them. 249
78. Treat Spare Moments Like Valuable Gemstones. 253
79. Learn The New Way. 256
80. When The Rules Don't Help, Throw Them Out. 259
81. To Be Your Best, Destress. 262
82. You Are What You Consistently Do. 265

A final thought. *272*
Acknowledgments. *273*
About Adam Albrecht *278*

INTRODUCTION

IN 2018 I visited Bangalore, India. The Weaponry, the advertising and idea agency I launched in 2016, was hired to tell the story of an impressive organization in Bangalore called SLK Global Solutions. The business had grown from fifty employees to 5000 in just over twelve years. As a business owner, I was intrigued by this kudzu-style growth. And I was determined to learn all I could from studying the organization.

When we arrived, we found a mammoth 500,000 square foot campus. It included multiple interconnected buildings, two giant cafeterias, a walking path through a forest garden, a rainwater reclamation system, and numerous large art installations. It also included a transportation system to move employees between home and work, operating like a school bus system, but for business.

The organization was far more remarkable than we expected. On our tour of their vast and modern facilities, I noticed something very interesting. Throughout the campus walls, framed posters featured the grandfather of the founding brothers Gopal and Parth Amin. Each of them highlighted one of the Grand Patriarch's core values.

The iconic businessman Shantanurao Laxmanrao Kirloskar was born in 1903, before the airplane, television, or computer. He died twenty-five years prior to my visit, but his approach to life and business is very much on display as a source of inspiration to this progressive organization's employees and visitors. And none of the posters was content to inspire with a simple, "hang in there, kitty!"

As I read each of the posters, I thought to myself, which of my core philosophies and values would inspire great success in my grandchildren and the organizations they run 100 years from now?

Sure, I had thought about my beliefs before. But I had never thought about capturing them as a source of guidance and inspiration for future generations. Or for future leaders who will guide and grow businesses years, decades, or even centuries from now.

To be clear, I don't know all there is to know about happiness and success. However, what I do know could serve as a solid foundation for others. Much of what I know to be true, I have learned by making mistakes. By collecting and sharing my learnings, I may be able to help others learn without having to make as many first-hand mistakes, which is the key to generational growth.

Do you have your own guidelines for happiness and success? Have you identified them, written them down, and shared them? In light of what I saw in India, it seems like a great idea for us all to identify our core beliefs and share them with our children, friends, and team members. You never know what you may inspire.

This book represents my attempt to gather my philosophies, organize my thoughts, and share my ideas with others I may never even meet. If I take my learnings to the grave, they will be lost forever. I'm hoping that doesn't happen. Because if others can profit from the lessons I have learned, they (and hopefully you) are likely to accomplish and learn far more than I have.

A NOTE ABOUT FORTUNE COOKIES

I HAVE ALWAYS been fascinated by fortune cookies. These crunchy, oddly folded treats that arrive at the end of a meal of American Chinese food are a gastronomic oddity. After all, most desserts are not hard and shattery. Those aren't particularly good dessert qualities as desserts go. It's a little like the dessert equivalent to the gum you find in a pack of baseball cards. In fact, you might not even know fortune cookies are edible unless someone told you they were.

The most interesting feature of the fortune cookie is not the cookie itself. Instead, it is the element that inspires its name, *fortune*. Once you crack into one of these cookies (I use the term loosely), you find a thin ribbon of paper with blue writing on it.

That tiny, unassuming piece of paper, ladies and gentle-readers, is your fortune. It is the key to your future. It contains either the advice you need to know or the direction you need to go. And this dessert-ish delivery vehicle is as close as most of us will ever come to discovering our genie in a bottle.

But how do you know it is *your* fortune?

The answer is simple. It is because *you* choose that fortune cookie. It is in your deciding that the fortune becomes yours.

Many years ago, I learned that you can not be handed a fortune cookie. Instead, they must be placed on the table for diners to select. That way, you are in control of choosing your own fortune. This choice is the key.

Just as fascinating as the cookie-human pairing process is the birth of the fortune itself. Where do these messages come from? The Universe? God? Fate? A fortune-teller?

It may come as a total surprise (or not), but human beings write these fortune cookie fortunes. These sacred writers are discovered and groomed for the job.

In this case, a young writer, perhaps right out of journalism school, embarks on a sacred journey that leads them to the fortune cookie job. It may be that they discovered their calling because they weren't funny enough for Laffy Taffy wrappers, not trivia-filled enough for Snapple caps, and not rebellious enough for graffiti.

I began my professional career as a young writer right out of college. Looking back at my journey now, I could easily have become a fortune cookie writer. I had recently graduated from the University of Wisconsin with a degree in journalism and psychology and was sleeping on the floor of my friends' Greg, T-Burgs, and Dunks apartment in Madison. I would have jumped at the opportunity to become a fortune cookie fortune writer. But alas, the call never came.

I can't help but think that, just as the cookie is chosen by its eater-reader, the fortune cookie writer may be selected by the same life force. I believe the universe magnetizes the writer to the fortune cookies. For many years, I believed that I was not the guy. I had accepted my reality. And in my heart and mind, I had moved on. I dedicated myself to learning everything possible about self-improvement, success, and positivity. Slowly but surely, the secrets of life have revealed themselves to me. In my enlightenment, I have come full circle. I am wiser, humbler, and in awe of all I have discovered.

Today, I have an overwhelming feeling that I am the chosen fortune cookie writer—the sharer of advice, wisdom, lessons, philosophy, and encouragement. But instead of writing strips of guidance onto thin pieces of paper and stuffing them into crunchy almond-flavored cookies, I am called to collect them in book form, to give the backstories. To elaborate on the reasons to believe in the fortunes. And to print them in a non-edible hardcover shell.

This book is my fortune cookie. Here I am sharing learnings, philosophy, and encouragement the universe has filtered through me to you. There are 80 fortunes in this book. And just like the pile of fortune cookies on the table, it is your job to find the one for you.

As you read this book, know that one of these messages is meant for you. It is the idea that will unlock doors for you and encourage you to keep moving forward. When you find it, you can stop and put the book away. Or pass the book along to the next reader to find their fortune. Or if you are curious, just as you might ask others at the table what their fortune says, you can read the entire book and know all of the other fortunes, too. The choice is up to you. Now let's start crackin!

CHAPTER 1

Constantly Upgrade Your Thinking.

HAVE YOU EVER wanted to be someone else? I have that feeling every day. I want to be a better version of myself. I want to be the me that I see in my head. *That* version of me is pretty amazing, which means that the 'today-me' is pretty lame by comparison.

But that doesn't discourage me. You won't find me feeling bad about myself—because I don't see myself as less-than.

I think of myself like an iPhone. I am constantly trying to create better versions of myself. Smarter, more powerful models of myself. I'm adding more features, capabilities, a longer battery, and more memory.

I read as if my future success depends on it. I listen to audiobooks while driving, podcasts about entrepreneurship while eating lunch, and podcasts about real estate investing while mowing the lawn. Each day I grow a little smarter, a little more capable, and a little closer to the version of *me* in my mind.

That vision of me as a better model of myself is why I work out. It's why I set goals. It's why I try new things that force me to grow. It's why I travel and see and do as much as possible. It is why I am excited to meet new people. All of these help me grow, expand, and improve.

As a business founder, I am growing and learning on the job every day. The resistance that entrepreneurship provides works just like the weights at a gym. They both help you develop a better, stronger version of yourself.

Don't be discouraged if the 'you' in your head is this year's iPhone and the real you feels like a flip phone. Keep moving. Keep iterating. Keep learning and growing.

Your improvements will come from better thinking. Better ideas inevitably lead to better actions, which lead to better outcomes. That's why accumulating knowledge has a positive compounding effect on your life, career, and personal impact.

Over the course of this book, you will discover new ideas to add to your mental weaponry. These ideas will help you improve in ways that will add to your happiness, your success, and your value to others. The goal of this book is to help you become a demonstrably better version of yourself than you are right now.

LAST BITE

There are thousands of versions of you yet to be. Each one gets stronger, smarter, and more capable. Each new model of you is even more valuable than the one before.

CHAPTER 2

The Best Way To Live A Great Life Is To Start At The End.

WHEN PRESIDENT GEORGE H.W. BUSH died, I watched the touching tributes during his presidential funeral at the National Cathedral in Washington, D.C. The highlight was from his son, President George W. Bush, whose eulogy honored his father, not as the 41st President and Commander in Chief, but as a caring family man.

W's thoughtful and tearful tribute brought back powerful memories of my grandfathers' funerals. My maternal grandfather, Kenneth Adam Sprau, (Grampy Sprau), a Navy veteran, died in 2009 when he was 92 years old. Three years earlier, in 2006, my paternal grandfather, Alton Archibald Albrecht died when he was 89. Both men left great human legacies. By that, I mean they left behind a lot of great humans as their legacies. In total, the two men had 21 children, which means that they dutifully obeyed God's command to go forth, be fruitful, and multiply.

Somehow, despite all those children and nearly 50 grandchildren, I was given the honor of delivering the eulogy for both my grandfathers. In full disclosure, no one else wanted the job. It is very difficult to talk at a funeral. I volunteered for the job. My family's only hesitation about me speaking at the funerals was that once I had a microphone and a captive audience, I might not stop.

Delivering a eulogy is an incredible honor and responsibility. And writing my first tribute for my Grandpa Albrecht also taught me one of the most important lessons of my life. Writing a eulogy forces you to look at an entire life, starting from the very end. It is how you complete the story of a human adventure on Earth. As I looked at Grandpa Albrecht's entire life, from the very end, it forced me to think about my life from the vantage point of its closing curtain.

Taking a eulogy viewpoint makes you think about your life as if it were a book, movie, or play. It makes you think about the plot, the characters, the obstacles, and the setbacks. You have to consider achievements, risks, rewards, and adventures. It forces you to think about your contributions and relationships, as well as your responsibilities and regrets. It makes you think about wasting time and making time and taking time and the scarcity of time.

As I wrote my Grandfather's eulogy, I realized that, sooner than I would like, I too will be done with my own story. And if I wanted to make a difference and create a great tale for someone else to tell, I had to do it now. I had to get busy doing the things I would regret not doing. I had to choose my own adventure. I had to live a story worth sharing.

I began seeing more value in each day. I started taking more pictures and documenting my journey. I began contacting friends and family more. I took on bigger challenges and made significant changes in my career. Within six months, I moved to a new state. I advanced two positions along my career path and nearly doubled my salary.

I planned more vacation time with my family instead of letting vacation days vanish at the end of the year. I had learned that those vacation days represented the pages of my story.

Following my Grandfather's funeral, I began writing down more plans and goals. In fact, I spent the last hour of my 39th year writing about all that I wanted to do in the decade ahead. It was one of the most important hours of my life because I wrote the story of my future in vivid detail. I could see it unfolding before me. And it was thrilling to see. I took the road less traveled. I did the scary things without fear. And my life became clear and amazing in that last hour before I hit 40.

I thought about unfinished business. I knew I would have serious regrets if I never tried to start an advertising agency because when I looked at my life from the end, that was a big part of my story. At that moment, my mind was set. I didn't dream of becoming an entrepreneur. I didn't wish to be an entrepreneur. I suddenly *was* an entrepreneur. I knew it to my core.

Two years later, I launched my agency. I called it The Weaponry. I envisioned my future and brought it to life. I started a blog to share my experience with others in hopes that they could also learn from my experience.

I shared my insights and observations whenever I thought they might provide value to others. I noticed that I kept offering this same piece of advice over and over: If you use the end perspective in your early decisions, you could actually steer the course of your life to align with your imagined life. This lesson was the greatest gift my grandfather ever gave me. It's exactly what I am doing. It's what I encourage you to do.

LAST BITE

By viewing your life from the end, you can clearly see what you could have done, and what you should have done. Do this while you can still do something about it, and it will turn your life into an epic story that is as big as your imagination.

CHAPTER 3

DREAMS HAVE A funny way of teaching us life lessons if we pay attention. I recently had a dream that I was invited to The Oscars. It was the opportunity of a lifetime, but I was indifferent about going. I made no real attempt to find appropriate attire. In fact, I figured some blue jeans and a decent shirt would do. Apparently, I had The Oscars confused with an Allman Brothers concert.

On the afternoon of the big event, I put on my far too casual Oscars ensemble. My wife walked in, looked me over, and said, "You are not seriously going to wear that..." But I *was* going to wear that. And I wasn't serious.

As I meandered towards the venue, not really caring if I got there, my mom called via FaceTime. She was thrilled about me going to the show until she saw my attire. She implored me to find something appropriate to wear.

I hung up with my mom and looked down, noticing that my very best clothes, including my tuxedo, had been laid at my feet. I realized that I would have to put on the tuxedo if I wanted to be let through the door of the Oscars. So, that's what I decided to do. Appropriately dressed, I restarted my journey towards the venue.

As I got closer to the event, I could hear an announcement warning, "you must be in your seat in five minutes, or you won't be permitted to enter." I began to panic and ran as hard as I could. But it was too late. I was too far away to make it to the show on time. Perfectly dressed but still unable to take in the event.

Then I woke up.

When I opened my eyes and realized it was all a dream, I quickly reflected on what I thought the dream meant. I realized it was a classic bad dream. It played off of my greatest concerns. I had a significant opportunity, and I blew it. I had everything I needed, served up on a silver platter, and I didn't realize it.

I didn't care. I didn't prepare. I wasn't listening to my wife and my mom, who represented the Universe. I caught lucky breaks, like having my right clothes show up when I needed them. (Of course, that is classic dream nonsense.) But still, I didn't act with urgency until it was far too late. The time had passed. The opportunity was gone. I blew it. As the hard-rocking Cinderella once sang, "You don't know what you got, till it's gone."

Not taking advantage of the great opportunities that come my way is an enduring fear. I worry about not recognizing the chances and advantages and lucky breaks I have gained. I am worried that

I won't hear the messages the Universe is sending. I have serious FOMO. But it is the vaccine that prevents me from contracting a boring life.

That same fear of missing out on your amazing life can serve as one of the most significant drivers in your life.

LAST BITE

Keep your senses tuned to the hints, inklings, and whispers the universe is sending to help you make your dreams come true. You will be offered great chances. But you have to take them.

CHAPTER 4

THERE ARE TWO kinds of people. We've heard this intro line many times before. We love to simplify the world's inhabitants this way because it offers an easy construct to think about complicated topics. I recently read one of these 'two-types-of-people' observations, and it wowed me with its simplicity and profundity.

> *"Some people prefer to say 'yes' and some people prefer to say 'no.' Those who say 'yes' are rewarded by the adventures they have. Those who say 'no' are rewarded by the safety they attain."*
> —Keith Johnstone, *Impro: Improvisation and the Theatre*

Wow! With this simple statement, Johnstone summarizes the difference between accepting and denying offers that come your way. Did you notice that both outcomes are positive? You either walk away with adventure or safety. Nobody goes home empty-handed. That's because life is like a good game show.

The key in deciding your path is to know which outcome you want most.

I am an emphatic *Yes-Man*. I like taking road trips without reservations. I am all-in on the adventure of life. I am an entrepreneur, and entrepreneurship is all about saying "yes". So is creativity. I see all of life's challenges through the 'Yes, and' lens. It truly makes every day adventurous, exciting, and full of new possibilities. I'm not saying being game for anything is better than safety. It's just better for me.

LAST BITE

If you prefer the safety, predictability, and peace of mind of your own home, embrace it unapologetically. If you prefer adventure, then embrace the bruises, wardrobe malfunctions, and flat tires as souvenirs from the trip.

CHAPTER 5

A Great Life Starts With A Great Plan.

YOU MUST PLAN your own career.

I recently spoke with a graduating college senior about what he planned to do following graduation. He said, "Honestly, I have no idea. I'll see what kind of opportunities come my way."

To me, this answer sounded like someone giving up on life or letting someone else write their story. It sounded like raising your hand to volunteer to be a pawn in someone else's chess game. (A pawn is a chess piece, right? Or is it another name for a shrimp?)

Without a plan of your own, you could end up in an industry you don't care about working a job that doesn't fulfill you. You risk getting tossed around like a plastic garbage bag in the wind, with no direction, like the memorable scene from *American Beauty*. You have to push to find work you are passionate about doing, even if the money isn't great. Not all rewards come in the form of cash.

Had I not planned my career, I would have ended up as an unhappy drug salesman. I studied psychology and journalism in college. But before graduation, I was approached by some pharmaceutical salespeople who were recruiting college athletes because, apparently, we are competitive people.

The money they offered me was twice what I would have earned in an entry-level job in Advertising. I declined their offer and held out for a creative role in advertising. It's because I had a plan. Pharmaceutical sales is a really great career choice for some people, but it did not fit into my plan. Not even a little. Not on a train. Not in the rain. Not with a fox.

I stayed focused and landed a good but low-paying job as a copywriter with a well-known advertising agency. Over the next 15 years, I progressed from a writer to Creative Director to Chief Creative Officer. Then, 19 years after I started my career, I launched my advertising and idea agency. It was all part of the plan. Like B.A. Baracus and Hannibal, I love it when a plan comes together.

Start working on your career and life plan today. Write down what you love to do. Write down what you are good at doing. Then find a way to get paid to do one of those things. Maybe you are already on that track. But maybe you are far away and heading in the wrong direction. You can turn around, but no one else can turn the wheel for you. That's your job.

If you are a new college grad, recently out of the military, or just released from prison, start your job search by thinking about your retirement. Plan your entire career with the end in mind. It's the best way to ensure you'll make the right decisions along the way. It will help you continue to educate yourself properly. With that plan in place, you will know when to introduce yourself to the right people. All of which will help you finish exactly where you want to be.

LAST BITE

You have to find a career that makes you happy. Your career will occupy 50% of your waking life. If you want to be happy in life, you have to be happy in your career. So make a plan and follow it. Don't follow the money. Because if you love what you do, everything else, including the money, will take care of itself.

CHAPTER 6

The Person Who Collects The Most Moments Of Bliss Wins.

A FEW YEARS ago, I took a vacation to the Pacific Northwest with my wife and three children. We visited amazing places, including Seattle, Mt. Rainer, Mount St. Helens, The Columbia River Gorge, Multnomah Falls, Cannon Beach, and Astoria. We visited Port Angeles and Forks, Washington, of *Twilight* fame. We also visited Vancouver Island in British Columbia, where I learned that one nation's Pacific Northwest lies directly below another nation's Pacific Southwest. #mindblown

That corner of the world is incredibly beautiful and picturesque. It explains why we saw so many people taking pictures. However, I noticed many people were taking pictures of themselves, even though they were not nearly as beautiful as the natural surroundings that surrounded them.

The selfie is an interesting cultural phenomenon. We take pictures of ourselves with people and things that we think will make us look cooler, more interesting, richer, or more attractive. Sure, selfies can help capture a memory. But the selfie snappers I encountered on vacation were missing the essence of the experience.

The goal is not to take a picture that makes it look like you are having a great experience. The key is to *have* an amazing, fulfilling, and rewarding experience.

The key to a great life is not to collect selfies. Instead, we should collect Self-A's. A Self-A is a way to reference our feelings of self-actualization. Self-actualization represents the highest rung on Abraham Maslow's hierarchy of needs. It is the ultimate state of human existence. It is the moment when we feel we have achieved our full potential. These are moments of completeness and bliss. But they only occur for a brief time. If you're not self-aware, you'll miss them.

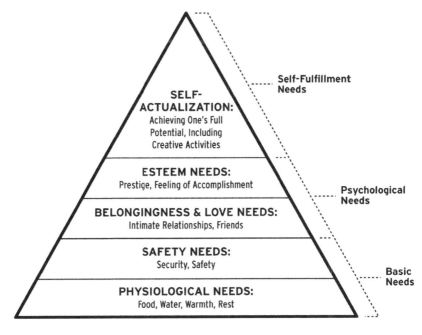

Maslow's Hierarchy of Needs

You can only experience Self-A if all your basic needs are met. You need food, water, shelter, sleep, safety, relationships, and confidence first. Once you collect all of those prerequisites, you can go for the bonus round of Self-A's. And when you experience self-actualization, you are literally living your dream.

Over the past three years, since beginning my entrepreneurial adventure and taking more control over my life, I have been experiencing more and more moments of Self-A. In fact, the increase in self-awareness is the most quantifiable and meaningful change in my life.

These moments occur at work, when I am ideating, when I am with my team, with friends, and when I am driving my John Deere lawn tractor. However, these magical moments of Self-A seem to happen most frequently when I am totally present on a family adventure.

On my recent visit to the Pacific Northwest, I noted that I was allowing myself to be absorbed into amazing moments while others were whipping out their mobile phones or selfie sticks to capture the moment. Stopping to capture a selfie kills your Self-A because you start focusing on the photo, not the feeling.

A NOTABLE NOTEBOOK IDEA

To fully enjoy these moments, try carrying a notebook to document the details of your Self-A's, answering the following questions:

- ▶ Where were you?
- ▶ Who were you with?
- ▶ What were you doing when you felt a moment as good, real, amazing, and as close to your dream as life ever gets?

By collecting notes on your Self-A's, you'll gain insights into how to experience even more of these priceless moments. And that is how you win in life.

LAST BITE

Don't settle for selfies. Don't aim to take pictures of yourself doing cool things in cool places with cool people. Focus on experiencing the moments. Aim for more moments when your reality feels as good as, if not better than, the dream. That feeling creates the best memory of all. Aim to feel that way as often as you can. You'll earn the reward of a life well lived. Not just a life well photographed.

CHAPTER 7

WHEN I WAS a kid, I knew about college. My parents both went to the University of Minnesota. Dartmouth College was across the street from my high school in Hanover, New Hampshire. Everyone from Hanover High School seemed to go to college. So there was never a question of whether or not I would go to college. It was just a matter of where. And whether or not I would get kicked out.

After high school, I went to the University of Wisconsin. I earned a double major in journalism and psychology. Following college, I had many friends who did even more schooling. They got master's degrees, went to law school or medical school.

I did none of those things. Instead, I began to self-educate. I started reading books, not just for entertainment, but for knowledge. I subscribed to various magazines and devoured them monthly. Eventually, I learned that devouring reading materials does not mean that you actually eat them. Once I discovered that, I began enjoying reading materials significantly more.

Over time, I started noticing an interesting trend when I read a book, article, or blog that I found valuable. Within it, I'd discover a reference to another book, article, blog, vlog, or podcast to add to my list of materials to explore. Not only would I find great value in the original material, but I would also find another reference to other worthwhile material to explore.

I began compiling a rich list of books, authors, blogs, and podcasts that continuously linked me to even more valuable new material. Like the required set of coursework you must take to earn a college degree, my self-directed readings began creating a unique and valuable path forward. They were like my own yellow brick road.

As I followed this chain of knowledge, it changed my life in profound ways. I didn't know it at the time, but my chain of knowledge created my coursework for entrepreneurship. Some of it was inspirational. Some of it was instructional. Each link added profound value.

In 2015 I began planning the launch of my advertising agency. Again, my readings and self-education prepared me well. I didn't need an MBA. Or a business coach. I just needed my self-directed chain of knowledge. And action.

In the spring of 2016, I launched my own business. And I discovered that to accomplish great and difficult feats, you don't have to go back to school, like Rodney Dangerfield. Or Billy Madison. You simply have to keep adding links to your own knowledge chain.

Sources that have provided strong links in my chain of knowledge:

Books

- *Rich Dad. Poor Dad* —Robert Kiyosaki
- *The Alchemist* —Paulo Coelho
- *Think And Grow Rich* —Napoleon Hill
- *The E-Myth* —Michael Gerber
- *Traction* —Gino Wickman
- *The Cashflow Quadrant* —Robert Kiyosaki
- *The 7 Habits of Highly Effective People* —Stephen R. Covey
- *The Hard Thing About Hard Things* —Ben Horowitz
- *Talent Is Overrated* —Geoff Colvin
- *Delivering Happiness* —Tony Hsieh
- *Call Me Ted* —Ted Turner
- *Pour Your Heart Into It* —Howard Schultz
- *The One Thing* —Gary Keller and Jay Papasan
- Every book written by John C. Maxwell
- Every book written by Jim Collins
- Every book written by Daniel Pink

Podcasts

- *How I Built This* —with Guy Raz
- *Masters of Scale* —with Reid Hoffman
- *Bigger Pockets* —with Brandon Turner and David Greene
- *Side Hustle School* —with Chris Guillebeau
- *Pretty Intense* —with Danica Patrick
- *The School of Greatness* —with Lewis Howes
- *The Mind Your Business Podcast* —with James Wedmore

Magazines

- *Inc.*
- *Fast Company*

LAST BITE

To become the best *You* that you can be, build your own chain of knowledge. Direct your own education. Add to it every day. It will empower you to do great things. Things that you alone are uniquely qualified to do. And please share what you discover with others. Because like Billy Madison, I still have a lot left to learn.

CHAPTER 8

I LOVE MY JOB. I thoroughly enjoy all aspects of my work. And not just the advertising specific stuff. I enjoy all of the businessy work I have to do as an entrepreneur. The problem solving I do is extremely rewarding. Every day feels like a game. Sometimes it's Monopoly. Sometimes it's Go Fish. And sometimes it's *The Running Man*.

As much as I love the work I do, one of my favorite parts of the workday is when we eat lunch and watch shows on Netflix. We watch a broad range of programming that either helps stimulate our thinking, makes us laugh, or both.

One of the programs we watched on Netflix at work is *The Repair Shop*, a reality show about a British repair shop. People bring antique treasures to the shop to have them restored to their former glory. The shop employs a furniture expert, a fabric expert, an art expert, an electronics expert, a clock expert, and more.

I love watching the experts at *The Repair Shop* work because they are all such great problem solvers. I learn from the ways they solve their problems.

In one memorable episode, an old Davenport desk came into the shop with a great deal of damage. One of the problems the team had to address was that the desk had drawers with locks but no keys to open them. Because the furniture expert really wanted to get in those drawers (snickering), he approached the clock and lock expert to see if he could help unlock the locked drawer. The clock and lock jock was happy to help.

He pulled out a large jar full of all kinds of random old keys, explaining that he has a large collection of old spare keys he uses to help unlock tricky locks. He then said that whenever he sees keys in an antique shop, he will always buy them to add to his collection so he can unlock even more locks in the future.

I instantly recognized that I do the same thing. I am always collecting keys. Except my keys don't come from antique shops. They come from books, magazines, and podcasts. They come from discussions with experts and from asking a lot of questions.

The keys that I collect don't go into a jar. I store them in my library, my notebooks, and the files of information in my head. My keys wait patiently for me to call on them to help me unlock the next problem I need to solve. And while I can't display them for the world to see, I know they are there. And the older I get, the more keys I have in my collection, which means I can unlock problems faster now than ever before.

LAST BITE

There are keys to unlocking problems everywhere. Find them in the things you read and the experts you meet. Discover them through experience and observation. So look for them. Collect them before you need them. And be prepared for whatever your world and your work send your way.

CHAPTER 9

THE LONG JUMP is one of my favorite track and field events. Not only is it entertaining to watch, but aside from the 100-meter dash, it is the easiest for an on-looker to relate to.

Long jumping is also one of the most useful skills in track and field. Imagine you are visiting Hawaii on vacation and a crack in the Earth opens up between you and your coconut drink. It would be really useful to be able to jump over the fissure and save your drink. I think that happened to Carl Lewis once.

I had several track teammates at the University of Wisconsin who were really good at the long jump. Here is a list of the notable Badger long jump marks when I was in school.

- Sonya Jenson: 19 feet 11 inches
- Heather Hyland: 20 feet 5 inches
- Jeremy Fischer: 24 feet 8 inches
- Maxwell Seales: 25 feet 2 inches
- Reggie Torian: 26 feet 2 inches

To fully appreciate how good these marks are, simply go out in your yard and see how far you can long jump today.

There Are Four Things To Love About The Long Jump:

1. The crowd clap.

The crowd watching a meet will clap in unison to motivate a jumper. The claps get faster and faster as the jumper sprints down the runway. I wish someone would do this for me at work as I fill out my timesheets.

2. The run.

It is exhilarating to watch a jumper accelerate towards the takeoff board. It's kind of like the countdown for a rocket launch.

3. The jump itself.

There is something primal and childlike about watching a human fly through the air self-propelled. It is pure fun. It reminds me of my adventures as a kid, jumping over creeks and jumping into piles of hay or leaves.

4. The landing (or what I call "the sanding").

What goes up must come down. Watching the jumper hit the ground again, usually in a spray of sand, is good dirty fun.

However, my favorite part of the long jump actually happens before any of that. It happens as a part of the competition day preparation that most people don't notice.

A long jumper doesn't just show up at the track, walk onto the runway, and start jumping. Instead, they have to find a starting point. To do that, they have to start at the end. They go to the takeoff board and work their way back down the runway from there to determine where they should begin their approach.

Some jumpers will stand on the takeoff board itself, with their back to the sandpit, and then run down the track, away from the takeoff point, counting their steps to find their starting point. Other jumpers use a tape measure. They set the end of the tape at the takeoff board and unreel it until they get to their preordained measurement. Then they mark that point on the runway as their starting point.

There is magic in that process that we can all learn from. The long jumper starts at the end of the run, the most critical point in the process, and then figures out, to the inch, where they need to start their run to hit that final point perfectly.

An interesting challenge here is that if you step an inch past the board in long jumping, your jump is considered a foul and disqualified. Yet every millimeter you are short of the board doesn't count towards your jump. Notice how I mixed the imperial and metric measurement systems? That's because I am bimeasural, which is like being bilingual, but not with linguals).

Before I launched my agency, I did the same thing long jumpers do. I put myself at the launch, imagining in great detail what my flight would look like once I finally jumped. Then I determined all of the steps I would need to take to launch the business properly.

I figured out how much time it would take me to create a launchable start-up. Then I started running, accelerating towards the launch point the whole time.

All of my steps have been purposeful to get me the results I am after. It took me eight months of planning from when I decided to launch The Weaponry until I was open for business. In less than three years, we were a multi-million dollar business and climbing rapidly. Just like I planned.

LAST BITE

To achieve great things, start where the story ends. Then work backwards. Because when you know your direction, your steps, and your takeoff point, you'll go as far as you can go. It's all in preparation. So put yourself in the best position to succeed. I'll be clapping for you the whole way.

CHAPTER 10

Get On Top Of Your Day Before Your Day Gets On Top Of You.

EVERY DAY STARTS full of potential. It is what you do with each of them that sets them apart. I am a card-carrying optimist. But I know that I will be dead long before I want to be. So making the most of each of the days I have is a top priority.

There is a saying that goes through my head every morning that helps me make each day great.

"Get on top of your day before your day gets on top of you."

I can't remember who said that. It may have been Anonymous or Unknown because those guys have said a lot of smart stuff. But this message hits my thought processor each morning and prompts me to write down the list of things I want to accomplish that day. Then I start cranking. And crossing things off. And feeling accomplished.

However, I don't intend for my lists to help me get the urgent things done. I couldn't ignore those things if I tried. The urgent tasks always demand attention. These lists are to ensure that I find time to focus on my pivotal electives.

Because of my daily list, I can find time for things like writing, mapping out a new business idea, connecting with friends, family members, or business contacts.

My lists help me prioritize exercise. And family time. If it's on my list, I will take a few minutes to work on a long-term project that could otherwise slide forever. The list helps me find time to learn. And time to be quiet. One of my favorite activities is what I call 'mental jogging' and this can only happen when I am quiet.

Today, I encourage you to get on top of your day. Picture the end of the day like an awards show that recognizes you for your Daytime Achievement (like a daily Lifetime Achievement award). What did they say you did that was so special?

Include the big pillars of the day on your daily list. But also add the quick little wins that you never seem to get to. And then get to it.

LAST BITE

You'll be amazed how five minutes can make the rest of your day so much more valuable. If you don't read this until 4 pm or 9 pm, try writing a list anyway. Many potentially unproductive days have been saved with a late list.

CHAPTER 11

Disappointment Is The Most Powerful Motivator.

I LOVE BEING an entrepreneur. After spending the first 19 years of my career working for ad agencies owned by other people, I decided to start my own business. That was in 2016. It was also a leap year, which is a good year to do anything because it gives you an additional twenty-four hours. (I tell this to presidential candidates and Olympic hopefuls all the time.)

Ever since I first launched my agency, people seem to think I am doing something impressive. Or daring. They are positive and supportive of my entrepreneurial adventure. I often hear from people who want to launch their own business. They tell me I was really brave to set out on my own. But when I analyze the driving force behind my leap into entrepreneurship, I can see that it was not bravery. Not even close.

I have wanted to run my own business since the beginning of my career. I envisioned myself as a business owner or business launcher-type guy. Whatever that meant. In fact, it was so clear to me that I would be an entrepreneur that after 15 years of working for other people, I considered myself a failure for not being a real entrepreneur.

Eventually, it was the disappointment and sense of dissatisfaction in myself that finally moved things forward. Don't get me wrong, I like myself. But I have a strong vision of my ideal self and whenever I am not acting in accordance with that vision, or I am too far off the pace I set in my head, it really bothers me. That disappointment and embarrassment is a powerful fuel we should guzzle regularly.

Most people never become so disappointed in themselves that it propels them forward. But that is an extremely valuable emotion. An injury to your pride is one of the best things that can happen to you. You just need to be incongruent with your self-perception. That feeling eventually pushes you forward like the other side of the magnet.

LAST BITE

Create a strong image of who you really are at your core. Think about it all the time. Eventually, you will get so fed up with not being that version of yourself that you will take drastic measures. It's in taking those drastic measures that the magic happens. And when you do, you will feel remarkably alive. Like you are no longer coasting through life. I hope that happens to you. Here's to you experiencing disappointment in motivating quantities.

CHAPTER 12

FOLLOWING SUPER BOWL LI in 2017, I expected to write a story about the commercials. But the next morning, I barely remembered them. The fragments I did recall were only because I was trying really, really hard to come up with something. As if I was being interrogated during a crime investigation. Um... there was the Skittles spot. Um... then Alfa Romeo showed up for some reason. Justin Timberlake referred to an old NSYNC song. And Terry Bradshaw was a mess.

I forgot about the commercials because of the game itself. It was hyper-relevant to my social circles and me because I grew up in New England as a huge Patriots fan. But I also lived and worked in Atlanta. I still have a house there. I have great love for my Atlantans and the way they embraced the Y'Albrechts. I didn't want either fan base to lose.

But I really wanted the Patriots to win.

If you were looking for entertainment, the game over-delivered. In fact, the game was the craziest sporting event I have ever watched at any level. I won't recap the entire game but I'll share a couple of inflection points.

Shortly after the opening kickoff, the score of the game was close. But things quickly went south like sweet tea. The Patriots were down by two touchdowns in the first few minutes. The TV announcers quickly pointed out that no team in Super Bowl history had ever come back from a fourteen point deficit. Gulp.

That concerned me, statistically. But come on, my team is the Pats! You know, Tom Brady, Malcolm Butler, Bill Belichick. They can make up fourteen points wicked fast. It was early in the game. I've seen this movie before.

But suddenly it was 21-0. Even the eternal optimist in me was discouraged going into halftime down 21-3.

It didn't get any better in the 3rd quarter. In fact, the Patriots were down by twenty-five points with just over two minutes to go in the 3rd quarter. That was two and a half times the largest lead any team had ever overcome in Super Bowl history. It was not good.

I felt like twelve-year-old Adam, watching my team get steamrolled by the 1985 Bears. I was having painful Steve Grogan, Tony Eason flashbacks. Even Bill Buckner made an appearance.

It was there, in the lopsided and thoroughly disappointing 3rd quarter, that an amazing Super Bowl statistic was born. It was a statistic with the potential to change your life if you let it. According to ESPN, "Atlanta had better than a 99.5% win probability when leading 28-3 in the 3rd quarter." Said another way, which I admit might be statistically impossible, "New England had less than a 0.5% win probability when trailing 28-3 in the 3rd quarter."

Yet, with not a second to spare, the Patriots began the most improbable come back. It included one of the most unbelievable catches in sports history, a last-moment touchdown and a rare two-point conversion to send the game to overtime. In sudden death overtime, the Patriots scored first, and completed the most remarkable big stage comeback in sports history.

I am not viewing the comeback as a Falcons fan. I don't see a letdown. Or a choke. Or an improbable loss.

I view the comeback as a Patriots fan. It was unbelievable in the truest sense of this overused word. And as the statistic shows, it was all but impossible.

But I also look at this crazy statistic outside of football. As a human. As a father. As a family member. As a business owner. I look at the 0.5% chance of winning as a friend of people battling terrible hardships, nasty diseases, demons, and addictions.

What happened in that game is a reason for the hopeless to hope. To believe the unbelievable. I have never purchased a copy of a championship game, but this game belongs in my library of reminders and inspirations. It may belong in yours, too.

Winning is hard. It requires you to never give up, never give out, and never give in. Let this game and this statistic serve as an inspiration when you pitch new business, cold-call, interview, and recruit. Let this game remind you to push harder when you are behind in revenue. When you are losing market share and when creditors are calling. There is always something you can do to turn things around.

LAST BITE

Never stop fighting whatever you are fighting. Remember to not give up on your dreams. Crazy things happen when people are crazy enough to keep trying. Odds are not facts. They are not rules. And the odds themselves do not cause the outcome. Actions do.

CHAPTER 13

Pressure Makes You More.

PRESSURE IS YOUR friend. It forces you to do things you might not have otherwise done. It forces you into action or keeps you moving when you might otherwise stop. As an entrepreneur, pressure has been my single greatest ally. (As I wrote the last line, my trusty MacBook Pro started singing, "What about me? It isn't fair…")

When I launched The Weaponry, I had a large mortgage, three kids, and a wife I really wanted to keep. That pressure forced me to make things work. Then, two months after establishing the company, I bought a second home and increased the pressure even more. Cue David Bowie.

Pressure gets me out of bed early every day. It forces me to focus throughout the workday. It keeps me fueled late at night when there are miles to go before I sleep. Because of the pressure, I am accomplishing more than ever before. I can't imagine what I wouldn't have done without it.

LAST BITE

Pressure is propulsion. Don't avoid it. Seek it out. It makes you run faster, farther, and with a greater sense of purpose. It forces you to consider all of your options and resources. It forces you to find solutions quickly. And it leads to results. Because there is no other option.

CHAPTER 14

IN 2019 FOR spring break, my family took a road trip across the Lone Star State. We hit Dallas, Fort Worth, Frisco, Plano, Waco, Austin, and San Antonio.

While we were in Dallas, we decided to see the site where John F. Kennedy was assassinated in 1963. It was interesting and sobering to see where this historical event occurred. We saw the infamous book depository (I admittedly still don't know what a book depository is). We saw the route JFK's motorcade was traveling in his last moments. We saw some grassiness. We saw some knolliness. And we saw the JFK Memorial, which made me think they must not have known what a good memorial looked like in 1963.

There are plenty of famous JFK quotes like, "Ask not what your country can do for you, ask what you can do for your country" and "We choose to go to the Moon in this decade and do the other things, not because they are easy, but because they are hard."

But when we browsed the JFK Museum store, I spotted a JFK quote I had never heard or read before. It instantly became my all time favorite from JFK.

"Things do not happen. They are made to happen."
— John F. Kennedy

This quote says everything there is to know about making an impact and achieving great things. It summarizes how you build and maintain a strong network of friends and family. It applies to everything from gardening, to creating a new law, to building a business from dust. These things don't just happen. You have to make them happen.

None of the things you want in life will happen on their own. They require energy and action. This reality is a warning and an inspiring call to action. It warns us that without action, you will get nothing and have nothing. But with action, you can have anything you are willing to work for.

LAST BITE

Action is everything. It is the difference between dreaming and doing. If you want something to happen, you have to force it and will it to happen through your vision, action, and energy. This wisdom applies to friendship, entrepreneurship, and every other ship in between.

CHAPTER 15

The Set Of Your Sails Determines The Way You Go.

MY GRAMPY SPRAU was born in 1916 in Meservey, Iowa. Meservey is a small farm town that mainly consisted of the twelve Sprau children in Grampy's family. I always thought the town sounded like someone was trying to say "Missouri" after too much Wild Turkey.

Grampy served in the Navy in the Pacific fleet during World War II. He came home (thank God), married my Grammy (thank God), and together they raised nine kids in Elkton, Minnesota. They also raised cattle and hogs and grew corn and soybeans. He farmed well into his eighties when they finally decided to retire and move to town.

Over the course of Grampy's life, he saw the world transform in unfathomable ways. When I once noted the changes he and his generation had witnessed, he said to me, "Adam, you could never understand what it was like to be us. We went from horse and buggy to putting a man on the moon."

Grampy was my witness to the greatest century of change in human history. He also taught me 98% of the swear words I know today.

Grampy was a library of fascinating sayings, songs, jokes, and poems. Some of it was purely silly. "I've got a dog, his name is Rover. He is nothing but a pup. He will stand up on his hind legs, if you hold his front legs up."

Some of what existed in Grampy's mental library was serious and profound. At a family gathering in Dublin, Ohio, when he was much closer to the end of his 92 years than the beginning, my uncle Jon asked Grampy to share the poem about the two ships. I had never heard the 'two ships' poem. And I bet Grampy hadn't recited the poem in the previous couple of decades. But Grampy immediately accessed 'Two Ships' in the jukebox in his head and performed it for our family.

"Tis The Set Of The Sail – Or – One Ship Sails East"

— Ella Wheeler Wilcox

> But to every mind there openeth,
> A way, and way, and away,
> A high soul climbs the highway,
> And the low soul gropes the low,
> And in between on the misty flats,
> The rest drift to and fro.

But to every man there openeth,
A high way and a low,
And every mind decideth,
The way his soul shall go.
One ship sails East,
And another West,
By the self-same winds that blow,
'Tis the set of the sails
And not the gales,
That tells the way we go.
Like the winds of the sea
Are the waves of time,
As we journey along through life,
'Tis the set of the soul,
That determines the goal,
And not the calm or the strife.

Hearing this poem was one of the most profound moments of my life. And not just because the poem itself is profound and inspiring. After Grampy recited the following passage, he broke down in tears.

"One ship sails East,
And another West,
By the self-same winds that blow,
'Tis the set of the sails
And not the gales,
That tells the way we go."

When a man who experienced more than eight decades of farm life, witnessed the greatest evolution in human history, enjoyed more than sixty years of marriage, lost his youngest son at nineteen years old in a farming accident, and participated in a worldwide war breaks down while reciting these words, you know they're important. It was the first and only time in my life I ever saw Grampy cry. I still think about that moment and that message when making important life decisions.

LAST BITE

Remember, "*tis* the set of the sails, and not the gales, that tells the way we go". So set your sails with purpose. And let all winds drive you toward your destination.

CHAPTER 16

MY TIME IS my most precious asset. Not because my time is any more important than anyone else's. It is certainly not. But just as Steve Miller's time keeps on "... slipping, slipping, slipping, into the future", I know that my finite time on Earth is steadily slipping away, too. Like sands through an hourglass. Literally. Yet, it is this scarcity of time that is *the* major motivating force in my life.

More and more, I find myself interrupting others as they recount their disappointments. I often crash pity parties to point out that time spent dwelling on the things that went wrong will not make them go right.

I am a problem solver both by nature and profession. As an entrepreneur and as a professional creative thinker, I view the constraints of any given situation simply as the rules that govern the solution. I have no time to relive something that went wrong in the past. All I care about is what I can do moving forward.

I find great value in the Serenity Prayer. If you don't know it, or don't know it by name, here it is:

"God, grant me the serenity to accept the things I cannot change, courage to change the things I can; and wisdom to know the difference."
– Reinhold Niebuhr

Many see this statement as a path to serenity. But I would have named this The Problem Solver's Prayer. Because what Reinhold is praying for is the essence of problem solving.

Problem solving is like conducting a science experiment. To find a great solution to the challenges you face, you must accept the constants and vary the variables until you get the results you are seeking.

Don't spend any time lamenting the constants. Instead, learn to accept the things you cannot change. Pour all of your time, energy, and thoughts into the things you can change. You could call that focusing on the positive. But it is really just focusing on the possible. It is not a rose-colored glasses outlook. It is focusing on reality. Because reality is full of positive possibilities.

LAST BITE

Memorize the Serenity Prayer. Accept the cold, hard realities of life. And spend all of your valuable and constantly diminishing time focusing on the amazing opportunities and possibilities that exist.

CHAPTER 17

Kick Start Your Day With A Smile.

YOUR FIRST ACT of the morning sets the tone for how your entire day will go. Some people cuddle with a cup of coffee. Some read. Others exercise. While still others begin their morning by repeatedly jabbing at the snooze button on their alarm clock as if they were picking a fight with the Pillsbury Doughboy.

My first act of the day is simple and, for me, more impactful than any of the above. When I wake up in the morning, the very first thing I do is smile. Instantly the day is good. It makes me feel like the new day is a game, and I am ready to play. I feel funny and playful. Because smiling to yourself in the dark for no reason is a funny thing to do. But it makes me feel good. And it puts me in the right frame of mind for the eighteen hour adventure ahead.

Like everyone else, I face challenges every day. I have three semi-domesticated children, a home that regularly throws me surprises, and a commute that I don't control. I own a business that comes with employees, contractors, clients, vendors, finances, insurance, and two landlords. And they all have the potential to hip check my plans each day.

But that first smile in the morning makes me feel like I have won the day before the sun even cracks the horizon. It sets the tone for everything else. It reminds me that funny things will happen that day, and it is up to me to see those events as humorous and not tragic, vengeful, or a clear sign of how much the universe hates me.

LAST BITE

Smiling is the easiest positive thing you'll do all day. Yet, it has the power to propel and protect you until you crawl back into bed at night. So, if you haven't smiled yet today, do it now.

CHAPTER 18

Put On A Smile Every Time You Dial.

HAVE YOU EVER thought about how you look when you make a phone call? It is easy to presume your appearance doesn't matter. After all, the person on the other end of the call can't see you. (Unless you are a Close Caller. Which is like a Close Talker, only you use your phone, because you can. Which is weird.)

Your appearance on a phone call *does* matter because how you look influences how you feel. Even if you are thousands of miles away, the person on the other end of the conversation will pick up on how you feel and it will influence what they send back to you.

When I make or take a phone call, I always put a smile on my face before I start talking. It magically brightens my mood. Smiling is the ultimate human happiness hack. You don't have to be happy to smile. You can simply smile to be happy.

Scientific studies have proven that your responses to questions are significantly more positive when you hold a pencil between your teeth the broad way. It forces your face to form a smile. And the forced smile has the same effect as the real thing. And while Marvin Gaye and Tammi Terrell would have you believe there ain't nothing like the real thing (baby), Guy Smiley and Happy Gilmore would disagree.

When you put a smile on your face before a phone call, it makes good things happen. It influences what you say, how you say it, and how you respond to your telephonic partner. It makes the call more enjoyable for the other person. It helps you overcome anxiousness when making an important call. And if the call goes poorly, well, it's easier to laugh it off if you are already in a smiling position.

LAST BITE

Before you pick up the phone, first pick up the corners of your mouth. Wearing a smile will positively impact everything about the call. It will make you sound warmer and more likable. It will influence the words you choose. It will leave a lasting impression on the person on the other end. It can even make them look forward to talking to you again.

If you want to try it now, put on a smile and call me at 614-256-2850. If I don't answer, leave a message and let me know you're practicing your smile call. And when I call you back, you can bet I'll be smiling, too.

CHAPTER 19

HOW MUCH TIME do you spend thinking about your thinking? I know that sounds like a funny question. But your thinking is the most important of all subjects to evaluate. Because your thinking determines your outcomes. It is a classic example of the *cause and effect* that you learned about in science class.

How it works:

Your thinking drives your actions. Your actions drive your results. Pretty simple, right? It's about to get even simpler.

Thinking → Actions → Results

What It Means:

Small thinking drives small actions, which lead to small results.

And the flip side, big thinking drives big actions, which lead to big results.

Most people spend far too much time on small thoughts. If you think only about your basic needs, your thinking will lead to very basic actions, and basic results.

However, thinking about your biggest goals and biggest dreams leads to your biggest actions. Which naturally leads to your biggest possible results. This is a big deal. ("Huge!" Like Julia Roberts's character boasted while shopping on Rodeo Drive with someone else's credit card.)

Think bigger thoughts. They lead to bigger actions. And that leads to bigger outcomes. And in a big country, dreams stay with you. I learned that in the 1980s.

- ▶ Think about changing the world for the better.
- ▶ Think about changing your community for the better.
- ▶ Think about changing an organization for the better.
- ▶ Think about changing your family for the better.
- ▶ Think about changing yourself for the better.
- ▶ Think about doing more of what you love.
- ▶ Think about making more money.
- ▶ Think about solving problems.
- ▶ Think about creating value.

LAST BITE

Big thinking and small thinking cost you the same amount. Nothing. The difference is that the return on small thinking is very small. And the return on big thinking is virtually limitless.

CHAPTER 20

Your Success Is Directly Related To Your Contribution.

I OWN A lot of books with the word 'rich' in the title. Among them, you'll find *Think and Grow Rich, Rich Dad Poor Dad, The Science of Getting Rich, The Richest Man in Town: The Twelve Commandments of Wealth, The Richest Man in Babylon,* and *Rich Like Them : My Door-to-Door Search for the Secrets of Wealth in America's Richest Neighborhoods.* I have bought so many books with the word "rich" in the title that Amazon now suggests books like *The Adventures of Richie Rich, Rich Desserts,* and *The Many Impressions of Rich Little.*

I like books with the word "rich" in them because they are really about success. They help you think and act in ways that help you accomplish great things. And those great things often attract money like magnets. Or magnates.

I consider the tips, tricks, and examples in these books more as important reminders than great "Aha!" moments. Nonetheless, there are certainly plenty of both in my library of riches.

If you want to know the most important point of all about getting rich, it is summarized in the following line:

> *"It is the value you bring to a company, an organization, indeed the universe, that ultimately determines your level of wealth."*
> — W. Randall Jones, *The Richest Man in Town: The Twelve Commandments of Wealth*

LAST BITE

If you want more, contribute more. If you want to earn more money, add more value. If you want more social capital, add more value. If you want more political capital, add more value.

CHAPTER 21

Assume The Defining Event Of Your Life Is Yet To Come.

JOHN MCCAIN WAS a remarkable American. When the long-serving senator from Arizona died of brain cancer, I received an alert on my mobile phone. I tapped on it and got a lengthy summation of his remarkable life. Much of his story was familiar, but one new fact about him jumped off the screen. (Figuratively, of course. There was no actual jumping.)

McCain was a Navy fighter pilot who was shot down, captured, imprisoned, and tortured for more than five years in Vietnam during the war. When he was released in 1973, he was determined that his experience as a POW would not be the defining event of his life.

The story is an excellent reminder that we shouldn't allow bad things to be what others remember about us. It is a call to push yourself to continuously do and be more. You can add so much to your life's story, career, and relationships that all the good minimizes the bad.

McCain's story also reminds us that, even in a life full of happiness and success, we can do more and be better. If you decide that the defining moment of your life has not yet happened, your next act can be even more significant than anything that has come before.

This perception is the best way to approach life.

Remember, you get better with time. Maybe not physically. But in all other ways. You gain wisdom, experience, insights, and connections. You begin to recognize great opportunities as you go. And you (usually) have more money to make more happen.

Bill Gates, one of the top five richest people on the planet and founder of Microsoft, may not be remembered for either of those things. It looks more and more like his greatest legacy may be from his philanthropic endeavors. The Bill and Melinda Gates Foundation has nearly wiped Polio off the planet and is tackling issues with clean water, sanitation, and renewable power. They are even working toward a cure for COVID-19.

LAST BITE

As long as you keep pushing yourself, your greatest days, the defining days of your life, are still ahead.

CHAPTER 22

Fill Your Attitude With Helium.

AFTER COLLECTING MORE than four decades worth of evidence, I have discovered that life is hard. My research reveals that life is hard at work, at home, in relationships, and even on vacation. No one is immune. And there is no cure (except that 80's band with Robert Smith).

Things go wrong all the time. Disappointment shows up repeatedly without an appointment. Things break. Bills pile up. Bills lose Super Bowls. And just when you think you are in the clear, something happens to remind you that you clearly are *not* in the clear.

I started The Weaponry in 2016. I have faced a constant stream of challenges, requirements, setbacks, and surprises. As an entrepreneur, you have to be ready for whatever craziness comes your way. Because it will come, and it will be crazy. Like marrying-a-Kardashian-crazy.

Since starting my entrepreneurial journey, I have surrounded myself with other entrepreneurs. I have noticed that these entrepreneurial rock stars have a special trait that enables them to succeed in the face of the constant barrage of adversity and in spite of the WTF-ity they inevitably face. That trait is human helium.

Helium is perhaps the most magical element on Earth because it floats! If you fill a balloon with helium, the balloon will float, too! Had Sir Issac Newton seen a helium balloon float skyward like he saw an apple fall earthward, he would have had a much tougher time discovering the laws of gravity. Helium always rises above the gravity of a situation. Your attitude can, too. If your attitude gets sunk by setbacks, your attitude is not an asset and needs a reset.

Don't focus on having a good attitude. Focus on having a *helium* attitude. It's a mindset, an approach, and an interpretation of the facts that allow you to rise above the circumstances. A helium attitude remains up, even when your plans fall down. Thus, it always provides the perspective that things will get better. This belief is a success imperative.

The helium attitude helps lift others, too. Someone needs to rise above the disappointment and frustration that we all inevitably face. The helium attitude bounces back quickly and offers other people a high point to focus on as they navigate forward. This reliance is why parents, leaders, teachers, and preachers need to fill their attitudes with as much helium as they can get.

LAST BITE

Life is unpredictable. One moment you feel like you are on top of the world. The next moment, you feel like the world is on top of you. But a helium attitude rises anyway. Don't let setbacks, curveballs, and negative people drag you down. Do what helium does, and just keep rising. Your attitude is everything in life. Make sure you fill it with the right fuel.

CHAPTER 23

SOME PEOPLE COLLECT stamps, art, or sports memorabilia. I collect rules of thumb. At this point, I have far more rules of thumb than I have thumbs. Which, upon further reflection, is not saying much. But I love a good, simple lens through which to view complex issues.

A few years ago, when I was looking to hire an Executive Creative Director in Atlanta, I found many interesting candidates. Michael Palma, the headhunter I was working with, posed an interesting question while we were discussing the merits of the various candidates. He asked, "Is the candidate's best five years in front of them or behind them?"

This startlingly simple logic is a great way to evaluate a job candidate because it boils a career down to trajectory. Is the candidate growing and learning and becoming more capable, more energetic, more inspired, more influential, more well-connected, and more valuable? Have they peaked? Have they begun coasting? Have they started living off of past successes? Are they still seeking out bigger challenges? Are they still hungry and feisty? (Are they still showering regularly?)

This query isn't just useful when evaluating job candidates. Its real power is that it is a great way to think about our own careers. And our own lives. I have sought out and surrounded myself with people who maintain an upward trajectory. I am inspired by people who continue to grow and challenge themselves to do, learn, and be more.

I started my business as part of a personal growth plan. I knew it was the next challenge that I needed to maintain my trajectory of growth, passion, and impact. As the business continues to grow and expand, it is clear that the best five years of my career are still ahead. If you have the right attitude, your best five years are still in front of you, too.

LAST BITE

Take a moment today to look at your big picture. Are you getting better? Are you pushing yourself? Are you taking on challenges that scare you? Are you maintaining a commitment to life-long learning and self-improvement? Are your interpersonal skills, maturity, and accountability improving? Is your network expanding and elevating? If not, it is time for you to spend more time working on you.

CHAPTER 24

DO YOU REGULARLY evaluate yourself? Most people only evaluate themselves and vow to course correct once per year. The start of a new year has a funny way of forcing us to take stock of what we have, how we look, the state of our careers, our relationships, and the effects of our bad habits. Then, once a year, we take actions to correct our course. But this *once a year course correction* approach is severely flawed. (Almost as flawed as my ability to properly fold fitted sheets.)

Imagine your ideal life as a road. All you have to do is drive on it. Now, imagine you find yourself veering ever so slightly towards the ditch or oncoming traffic. When should you make a course correction? The obvious answer is that you should course correct as soon as you recognize you are veering! But what if you don't? What if you only steer once a year?

If you only make a course correction once a year, you will only ever make a maximum of a hundred adjustments. (And that's making some generous assumptions about your longevity and the age at which you scribbled your first New Year's resolution.)

At just a hundred adjustments over a lifetime, one of two things happen. You either veer far off course each year, or you travel really (really, really) slowly to prevent winding up in the ditch before the end of the year. Either way, a hundred lifetime corrections severely limit your ability to travel your ideal path.

Driver Safety Quiz:

Question: How often do you need to make subtle adjustments when driving an actual car on an actual road?

Answer: Every few seconds.

It is simple math. An annual evaluation and course correction will allow you hundred chances to follow your true path. A monthly correction will provide you with 1,200 chances. Weekly evaluations will provide 5,200 lifetime adjustments. Daily course correction will provide you with 36,500 chances to travel your true path (plus roughly twenty-five leap days, which you can use as you please).

I'm not saying you need to course correct every day. I'm also not saying you *shouldn't*. A weekly or monthly inventory check will dramatically improve your odds of attaining your goals and living the life of your ideal design.

LAST BITE

Don't wait until the end of the year. Start by re-evaluating your course today. If you are not heading towards your true north, make the necessary adjustments now. Keep recalibrating. Steer yourself exactly where you want to go.

CHAPTER 25

Always Know Where You Are On Your Journey.

LABOR DAY IS YOUR national holiday. It is a day dedicated to honoring the work you do. Yes, you!

According to The U.S. Department of Labor, the holiday was created to recognize the contributions that workers have made to the strength, prosperity, and well-being of our country.

Labor Day is a great time to take the day off, eat a hotdog, drink a Miller Lite, and blow off some steam by throwing some bags in a hole. It also is the perfect day for your annual career evaluation. It's like a mammogram or prostate check for your career. Only you get to keep your clothes on (if you want).

Careers are long and complicated journeys. Along the way, we often become so consumed with our daily work that we don't think about the big picture. It is easy to focus on the tasks and lose sight of the career.

At the beginning of your career, it is important to map out your ideal course.

You should know what types of roles, positions, and titles you expect to have along the way. Think about the types of companies you want to work for and the kinds of skills and experiences you are expected to accumulate along the way. If you haven't done this yet, do it now. Establish all the things you want to accomplish in your career *and* visualize what the end looks like now.

I have had a clear vision of my entire career path from the beginning. Because I charted the path early, I always knew where I was headed and what I needed to do next to get there. But even with this vision in place, it can be easy to linger too long in one place. Like Dorothy, Toto, and the Cowardly Lion in the field of poppies, we can grow comfortable, complacent, and sleepy.

Luckily for me, my wife Dawn always seems to know when it has been too long since I have checked the progress on my career map. At those times, she poses these two simple questions:

1. Are you where you want to be?
2. Where are you going next?

These two navigational questions have been extremely helpful to me. Here is how they can be helpful to you, too.

Six Ways Navigation Questions Help Your Career:

1. They remind you that you have a career plan (if you haven't written yours down, do it now).
2. They make you cognizant of the passing of time.

3. They remind you of your valuable accumulation of experience and abilities.
4. They remind you that if you want to accomplish everything in your plan, you need to keep moving.
5. They help you rise above your current day-to-day work to see your entire career and how much of it is yet unwritten. (Right, Natasha Bedingfield?)
6. They remind you that if you don't start writing the next chapter, there will be no next chapter. There will be no rising drama and no great triumph. There will be no cray-cray challenge that tests your fortitude. Your career story will end here, in this chapter. That is perfectly acceptable if you have accomplished everything in your plan. I have not.

CAREER CHECK-IN HISTORY:

Labor Day 2015

My career evaluation was full of excitement and potential. But only if I followed through with the plan and plunged into entrepreneurship, which was the next square on my Career CandyLand board game. At the time, I was deep into my plans for starting my advertising agency. But I still had to take the entrepreneurial leap, which I knew would be the most difficult part of my entire career journey.

Labor Day 2016

I had officially left my job and launched The Weaponry in April and by Labor Day, we had already amassed eight clients. I was learning. We were growing. I was on course.

Labor Day 2017

I couldn't have been happier. I loved what I was doing. I love what we were building at The Weaponry. I had a great team of co-workers. I loved the clients we had been honored to help. We worked with more than twenty great brands in the United States and Canada. It was the most exciting and rewarding chapter of my career. But I wouldn't have gotten to it if I had not regularly pondered where I stood in my career and where I wanted to go next.

LAST BITE

Find the next step towards the type of success you've always wanted. Take the steps that add new, more interesting chapters to your life story. Don't just coast through each year trying not to get fired. If you stop evaluating for too long, it becomes too late. The game is over. The book is done, and no one wants to read it. But if you chart your progress and refocus regularly, you'll have a book to be proud of.

CHAPTER 26

TO ACHIEVE GREAT things, you have to start with a great vision. It is the key to growth and transformation. It is how I have developed from a silly young advertising copywriter into the CEO and owner of a multi-million dollar company.

One of my favorite things about The Weaponry is our quarterly team meeting. I open each one by saying something ridiculous. And it goes like this:

"The Weaponry is a (insert ridiculously large revenue number) business, with (insert ridiculously large number) offices, and (insert ridiculously large number) employees. Our job is to close the gap between the ideal, fully formed version of The Weaponry I just described and The Weaponry that exists today."

We work as a team to identify the most important things our agency must add, remove, implement, enhance, or change to close the gap. The intent is to develop who we are today into that ideal vision.

However, we don't just discuss our vision in quarterly meetings. We constantly compare ourselves to the ideal image of the business. It's our version of "What Would Jesus Do?". When making decisions about everything from hiring to copier machines to our website and business development, we continually ask, "What Would The Fully-Formed, Fully-Realized Version of The Weaponry Do?" You know, the classic WWTFFFRVOTWD?

By creating a strong, tangible, and detailed vision of your future self, you have a standard to guide your decision-making. For example, ask yourself, "How does *Future-State-You* handle performance reviews?" Or "How does Future-State-You develop a pipeline of new business opportunities?" Or "How does future-state-you take vacations?"

When you ask such questions regularly, you'll quickly find the answers sitting at the top of the search results. That's because you've optimized your ideal state for your mental search engine.

This envisioning approach is not just for businesses. It works for individuals, too. By creating a clear image of your future self, you always have a great model to follow. When you stand back-to-back with your future self, it is easy to see how you stack up against each other. You can easily recognize the gaps in knowledge, professionalism, experience, patience, or reliability you need to close. The comparison forces you to focus your efforts on acquiring new knowledge and skills. It may even encourage you to update your wardrobe.

LAST BITE

The only person you should be jealous of is *fully-formed-you*. It is the only comparison that matters. And the only one that you can control.

CHAPTER 27

Focus On What You Want The Most.

SETH ROGEN IS a funny guy. He is so amusing that Jerry Seinfeld invited him to appear on *Comedians In Cars Getting Coffee (CICGC)*. You know you are funny when Seinfeld wants to drink and drive with you. And, of course, ask you about comedy.

On *CICGC*, Rogen told the story of how he started performing stand-up comedy when he was fifteen years old in Vancouver. (I'm not sure how old fifteen in Canadian years translates to in American years, but I think it's still pretty young.) He regularly performed stand-up several times a week until he was eighteen years old.

Rogen recalled one particular joke from a comedian that still stands out to him today. He shared the joke with Jerry Seinfeld (and me as I eavesdropped on their car conversation from home). And now I'm sharing it with you.

"I wanted to be a boxer until I met someone who reeeeeallly wanted to be a boxer."
— Unknown

Rogen shared that line, not just because it was funny and interesting but to provide insight into his next chapter. After high school, he moved to Los Angeles, where he planned to pursue his stand-up comedy career. But upon being introduced to the highly competitive L.A. stand-up scene, he concluded:

"I wanted to be a stand-up comedian until I met people who reeeeeallly wanted to be stand-up comedians."
— Seth Rogen

I love this story. There are things we think we want until we see how competitive it *reeeeeallly* is. Or how hard it is. Or how good other people are at it. Or how hard people will punch you in the face if you stand in front of them.

To determine if you *reeeeeallly* want to take on your next challenge, ask yourself these five questions:

1. Do you *honestly* want to do this thing?
2. How committed are you, *reeeeeallly*?
3. Are you prepared to compete with others who *reeeeeallly* want what you want?
4. Are you ready to sacrifice?
5. Are you willing to endure the pain required to achieve your goal to avoid the pain of having not achieved it?

When I first started planning to launch the agency, I had to ask myself these five questions. And the answer to all of them was a loud and resounding *yes!* (Is there such a thing as a quiet and resounding *yes*? Maybe if Clint Eastwood says it.)

I was committed to succeeding. I was committed to the pain. I was committed to the sacrifice. I was committed to fighting and competing. And I am just as committed today as I was on day one.

To be clear, it's okay if the answer to any of the questions above is "no". That means the thing you think you want is not the thing you actually want. That is good. It frees you up to discover what you want most, just like Seth Rogen did. Among other things, he went on to write the hit movie *Superbad*, star in *Knocked Up* and *The 40-Year-Old Virgin*, and direct *This Is the End*.

LAST BITE

You will always be most successful at the things you want the most. Be honest with yourself. Don't waste time with things you wish you could do or that you are sort of into. Instead, find a career, adventure, or cause that you can go all-in on. Going all-in is the most rewarding way to go. It will lead you to your greatest potential for success. Find your thing and fully commit. It's the best way to enjoy what you do every day. (*Reeeeeallly*).

CHAPTER 28

WORKING AT AN advertising agency is like being in college your entire career. Not just because silliness is omnipresent. But because you are constantly learning new things. Every new client represents a new product, service, or entire industry to learn. I have discovered more about the world by working in advertising than I did in college. (And I learned a lot in college.)

One of the clients from which I have learned a great deal is StayWell. This company pioneered corporate wellness programs more than forty years ago. The effectiveness of their program is rooted in the proven science of behavior change. Today, StayWell works with many of the best companies in America, helping to improve employees' lives every day.

During a video shoot with StayWell's health and wellness coaches, I heard inspiring stories of how the coaches had a transformational impact on the lives of those they coached. There was one particular story that hit me in my 'profunditude' receptors.

THE STORY

The last coach of the day told us a story about a man she had coached. He had a variety of health and lifestyle issues, one of which was that he was an enthusiastic smoker. I translated that observation to mean that he liked standing outside, alone, by a back door, even when it was freezing out.

The man knew he should quit. The warning labels on the cigarette packs made it clear that he would die if he smoked the cigarettes. But he had not yet summoned the resolve and created a master plan to make it happen.

One day, the coach suggested that the man try just one day without cigarettes. It was a pretty small challenge. Much easier than really quitting. The man tried it. And the man succeeded.

At the end of the day, he realized that it had been several decades since he had gone a whole day without a cigarette. He was very excited about his big day and he wondered if he could do it again the next day.

That was two years ago, and he hasn't smoked a cigarette since.

Too often, we think we have to do something monumental to get results. That is poppycock. All you have to do is start. Do something. Anything. The littlest step in the right direction is progress. It helps you build momentum. Because success builds like a snowball. It always starts small. But as it rolls, it has the potential to become massive.

I always wanted to start an advertising agency, but entrepreneurship seemed daunting until I broke it down into small, simple steps. I simply started taking one small step after another and today I'm the Founder and CEO of The Weaponry. We have numerous employees, two locations, and more than twenty clients from coast to coast. It all started with one small step.

LAST BITE

All big accomplishments start with small steps. Take the smallest, easiest step forward. You'll find that it is so easy that you can't help but take another step forward. When you do, the next one will reveal itself. And when it does, you take that step, too. You don't have to be prepared for the whole journey. You only have to be prepared for the next small step. Knowing and believing this truth is the first and most important step of all.

CHAPTER 29

Forget Everything That Doesn't Help You Win.

I LOVE A good quote. In fact, I consider my ability to be influenced by a good quote to be one of my greatest assets. I love the way a powerful statement can summarize a complicated concept in a simple, memorable way. I regularly add these little gems to my personal guidebook and pull them out to remind myself how to respond to challenging situations like starting a new business or surviving Atlanta traffic.

I recently came across a great quote from Nike co-founder Phil Knight. In his book *Shoe Dog*, Knight shares the challenges he faced when fighting for U.S. distribution rights of the Japanese-made Onitsuka Tiger running shoes in the early 1960s. He was in a showdown with a formidable opponent who also wanted exclusive distribution rights. And that meant that he was going to have to compete to win.

Knight recounts his philosophy on competing in the book with the following statement:

> *"The art of competing, I'd learned from track, was the art of forgetting, and I now reminded myself of that fact. You must forget your limits. You must forget your doubts, your pain, your past."*
> — Phil Knight, *Shoe Dog*

To compete, you must forget. When you compete, you can't let past performances determine future outcomes. You have to expect that the next performance will produce the desired outcome. It's true in business. And it's true in your personal life.

Selective amnesia is a powerful thing. It gets you to try again. Even if you have lost, failed, or suffered in the past, you can't let a loss win. Forget it and keep going. Get back up. Dust yourself off (if you live somewhere dusty), then try again.

LAST BITE

Forget your failures. Forget your rejections. Forget the losses, the suffering, the pain, and the disappointment. Remember, every chance is an opportunity for a new and better outcome.

CHAPTER 30

WE ALL EXPERIENCE life in three modes:

1. Growth Mode
2. Maintenance Mode
3. Atrophy Mode

These modes are not sequential. You can shift from one to another in any order you choose. Read a book, and you are in Growth Mode. Rest on your laurels, and you are in Atrophy Mode. Brush your teeth, and you are in Maintenance Mode. (Listen to some 80s English electronic music, and you are in Depeche Mode.)

Right now, I am spending as much time as I can in Growth Mode. I am reading to learn. I'm working out regularly. I am expanding my business, which pushes me to grow every day.

To push for more growth, I am soaking up as much as I can about inventors and pioneers. I've studied Walt Disney, Lewis and Clark, the team at Pixar, and Ernest Shackleton.

Currently, I am studying and greatly inspired by Orville and Wilbur Wright. Notice I say that I am *studying* them, not reading about them. You can read simply for entertainment or to kill time. I'm studying because I am hungry to learn and grow.

For those who aren't up to date on turn-of-the-last-century trivia, here's a quick lesson. Orville and Wilbur Wright invented the airplane and it changed the world forever. If it weren't for them, you wouldn't be able to complain about the lack of legroom or that spotty in-flight wi-fi as you jet across all of America in a mere six hours.

One of the things that stood out to me about the Wrights was their highly pragmatic approach to their own growth and learning. Today, you and I can use their strategy to develop our personal and professional breakthroughs.

To learn and grow like the Wright Brothers, consider the following excerpt from a speech Double Dubs (my nickname for Wilbur Wright) gave to a group of engineers in Chicago:

"Now, there are two ways of learning to ride a fractious horse: One is to get on him and learn by actual practice how each motion and trick may be best met; the other is to sit on a fence and watch the beast a while, and then retire to the house and at leisure figure out the best way of overcoming his jumps and kicks. The latter system is the safest, but the former, on the whole, turns out the larger proportion of good riders. It is very much the same in learning

to ride a flying machine; if you are looking for perfect safety, you will do well to sit on a fence and watch the birds; but if you really wish to learn, you must mount a machine and become acquainted with its tricks by actual trial."
— Wilbur Wright, 1901

You may not be trying to ride a fractious horse or a flying machine, but Wilbur's approach holds true for you, too. You can study that challenge in front of you from the comfort of your couch. You can read about it, talk about it and watch other people do it. But if you really want to learn how to do it yourself, you have to climb aboard your flying machine and master it through trial and error.

That method is how I started The Weaponry. I read and studied and tried to prepare ahead of time. But eventually, I had to jump in the cockpit, pull back on the yoke and start messing with the controls. I'm learning by doing. And I'm learning faster than I ever could have from a book or a class.

The Growth Mode approach is the key for learning anything. You learn how to kayak, juggle, write code, start a nonprofit, lead, cook, invest, or speed eat hot dogs by doing. Experience is the greatest teacher. Don't be afraid to make mistakes. Mistakes help you course correct and keep you moving forward.

Don't settle for Maintenance Mode and avoid Atrophy Mode at all costs. Keep growing, not by watching or reading, but by doing. Get off the fence and climb aboard your horse, bicycle, or flying machine today. Keep at it until you get it right. Just like the Wrights.

LAST BITE

Trying will teach you how. Action is the best educator. You'll limit your learning if you stay on the sidelines.

CHAPTER 31

Celebrate Your Attempts.

I HATE THE word "failure." In my book, failure is the real "F"-word. So, why the F has failure become so popular lately? Organizational leaders, motivational books, and quasi-business coaches are encouraging us to embrace our failures. They tell us to fail fast and fail more often. They say that if you are not failing, you are not pushing yourself enough. I fail to understand this thinking. In fact, I don't place any value on failures.

When I set out to create my advertising agency, I expected it would be a lot of hard work. I expected that I would be underprepared for challenges I'd face. But one of the best things I did from the beginning of my entrepreneurial adventure was to give myself permission to be an amateur.

As an amateur, I have valued one thing above all else; the attempt. The attempt is the action that creates all possibilities of success. Failure is nothing more than a result of having attempted. Failure by itself does not lead to success. Never forget that.

Newton's first law of motion says that a body at rest will remain at rest. *True dat*, Sir Isaac! Do you know what that means? A body at rest does not start a business. It does not change paradigms. It doesn't invent new products or services. A body at rest does not create a magnetic culture. It does not develop a force that helps businesses thrive. A body at rest does not lead a company in sales. It does not create a positive impact on friends, families, and communities. The only thing a body at rest does is remain at rest. And that is tragic.

Action is everything. As long as I am taking action, I can give myself credit. Every action gets me closer to success. Action is energy. Action is the possibility maker. Action is the seed of accomplishment. Remember the old saying that "sex is hereditary"? (If your parents didn't have sex, chances are you won't either.)

If you don't take action, none of your dreams will materialize.

Life is like golf. To get the ball from the tee into the hole, you need action. That, my friends, comes from you swinging the club. If you are too lazy or too afraid to swing the club, you will never get the ball in the hole. Simply by swinging the club, you have given yourself a chance to succeed.

As I grow the company, I put a premium on action. I place a high value on simply taking one step after another. If the steps are off, or fruitless, or inflict pain or damage, that's okay. The key is to learn, correct, and act again.

It was either Steve Perry or Lao Tzu who said, "A journey of a thousand miles begins with a single step." And importantly, every step of the journey is a single step taken.

You'll have some missteps along the way that will ultimately make your journey 1001 miles, or 1110 miles, or 2000 miles. That's okay. Missteps aren't failures. They're action.

LAST BITE

Take the first action. Take the second action. Then keep going. That's how it happens. Don't embrace failure. Embrace the action that created the possibility.

CHAPTER 32

Start. And Improve From There.

I LOVE TRACK and field. I first got involved in the sport as a freshman in high school, mostly because I was terrible at baseball. But also because it was co-ed. And, I thought the fact that it was a no-cut sport significantly improved my chances of actually making the team.

I have competed in almost every track and field event under two miles. My athletic resumé includes the 100 meter dash, 400 meter dash, 1600 meter run, 110 meter hurdles, high jump, long jump, shot put, discus, javelin, hammer, 35-pound weight, 4×100 meter relay, 4×400 meter relay, and even the pole vault (which I approached more like the high jump with a stick).

I enjoyed every event I ever competed in. I loved the energy and atmosphere at track meets large and small. From the small summer all-comer meets to the Drake Relays and the Mt. Sac Invitational where 30,000 and 40,000 fans packed the stands.

The most important and impactful event in a track athlete's career is the second meet. In your first meet, you set a baseline. Then you walk into your second meet with a time, distance, or height to beat. And most of the time, the results are a rewarding step forward from the first meet.

However, in track and field, every result is measured in minutes and seconds, or feet and inches. Those metrics mean that your linear progression is clear and quantifiable. Improvement in the second meet gets you thinking about the third. It makes you do things like practice more, train harder, lift more weights, warm up smarter, and find better hype music. You start wondering just how much better you can get. You plant, fertilize, and water the seeds of self-improvement in that crucial second meet.

This principle is not limited to track and field. It's a life thing that applies to our careers, relationships, responsibilities, and hobbies.

Our first attempt simply sets a baseline. The second time we do anything, we start the improvement process. It's true of presenting a closing argument in court, hiring good employees, and folding fitted sheets.

As you pour more energy, time, and focus into any activity, you get better and better. And as you improve, remember that first attempt. Recognize how far you have come since you first started. It is one of the most enjoyable and rewarding reflections you will ever experience.

LAST BITE

Don't be afraid to try something new because you think you will be bad at it. You *will* be bad at it. Or at least you will be the worst you will ever be. But that first attempt creates a starting point. The climb from there is both exciting and rewarding.

CHAPTER 33

The Path To Great Achievement Is Lined With Fake Deadlines.

YOU HAVE DREAMS. I know you do. You have visions of a future that is better than today. In your dream state, you have a better job, a more exciting career, or your own thriving business. You have lost weight, gained fame, made a fortune, and crossed off everything on your bucket list. You, my friend, are Forrest Gumping.

The hardest part about making your dreams come true is that dreams are electives. They are not requirements. Unlike taxes, you can put dreams off forever without getting into any trouble. The downside is that when you die, your dreams die, too. And as you go to your final resting place, your unrealized dreams will be left behind, still in their wrappers.

The key to bringing your dreams to life is simple. Create fake deadlines. You have to convert your elective activities into required activities, complete with a due date.

How do you create fake deadlines? You just make them up. It's the same way we created leprechauns, unicorns, and the Backstreet Boys. You simply create a fake timeline to make your dreams a reality. Then you "deadline" your way forward because deadlines are key to keeping your dreams alive.

On the eve of my 40th birthday, I set a series of goals and fake deadlines for myself. One of my goals was to start an advertising agency. Less than three years later, I formed The Weaponry. A fake deadline gave my entrepreneurial dream a sense of urgency. That urgency forced me to make it a priority and give it the necessary attention to meet the deadline and make it a reality.

At the beginning of every quarter, we set "rocks" (goals) that we must accomplish within 90 days. Of course, we make up that 90-day deadline, but it creates urgency and forces us into action. It gamifies our efforts and keeps us moving forward and improving as an organization.

I publish three new posts to my Adam Albrecht blog every week. I do it to share the experiences, insights, and wisdom I've gained from building The Weaponry. I share life lessons, inspiration, motivation, and proven approaches to self-improvement.

No one is making me write. No one else is telling me that a new post needs to go live every Tuesday, Thursday, and Sunday. But that's what my self-imposed deadlines demand. So I deliver. As a result, my readership steadily increases by 50% each year.

Fake deadlines make things happen. They are the genuine keys to progress. To accomplish something important to you, start by setting an arbitrary deadline to get started. Then set a fake deadline for completion. And set lots of fake deadlines to meet important and aggressive milestones along the way. Without deadlines (real or fake), dreams die. That's just reality. Don't let it happen to you. Set your fake deadline today. Tick Tock. Tick Tock. Tick Tock.

LAST BITE

Nothing is important until it has a deadline.

CHAPTER 34

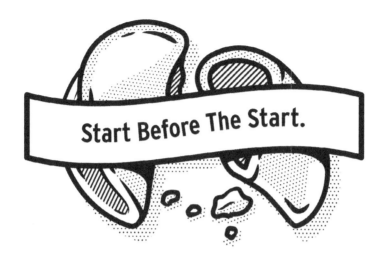

Start Before The Start.

WHEN I SET my yearly goals, I cheat to attain them. I fully admit it. But it's not the kind of cheating that hurts anyone else. Actually, it's not the kind of cheating that hurts anyone at all. But it certainly gives me a major advantage. And I don't feel the least bit bad about it.

Most people set their goals for the year and begin working toward them on January 1st. Or maybe they start January 2nd, depending on when the holidays fall. Or maybe on January 3rd, depending on which college football bowl games are on TV on the 1st and 2nd. Then, despite the fact that we all have 365 days to accomplish our annual goals, most people lose their momentum before the end of the first month.

I don't want to be one of those people, so I give myself every advantage possible. I noticed long ago that no one calls you for a false start if you start working towards your annual goals early. So I cheat. I start working on my goals for the upcoming year before the current year is over.

For example, I start working on my fitness goals for the next year on Thanksgiving. I enjoy contrarian thinking. For me, Thanksgiving is a cue to get fitter, not fatter. That way, I start the new year with a healthy routine already formed.

My wife Dawn and I begin planning our travel adventures for the coming year as soon as we have taken our final trip of the current year. That last trip typically happens right before Labor Day (because kids ruin everything). I discovered that when I waited too long to plan my vacations, they didn't get planned at all. And that meant they didn't happen. So now we schedule adventures early, and we get more out of them.

For the same reasons I make fitness and travel plans early, I clearly define my professional goals well before January 1st. In business, your current year's trajectory is highly influenced by what you did in the fourth quarter of the prior year.

When you add new business in the Fall, you start benefiting from it right away, at the beginning of the first quarter. And it pays out all year long. In contrast, new opportunities that surface in the first quarter may not bear any fruit until the second, third, or fourth quarter. This shorter runway means that a piece of business worth $1 million, $100,000, or $1000 over the course of 12 months will only be worth a fraction of that in the following calendar year.

Even though I launched The Weaponry in the Spring of 2016, I began planning my business in August of 2015. I took on freelance projects starting in October of 2015. The income from those projects provided the seed money to start the agency. My early start was key to a successful launch. You can do the same thing in any area of your life. And when you do, you'll find that it stacks the deck in your favor.

LAST BITE

If you want to be great, you can't wait.

CHAPTER 35

Early Mornings Beat Late Nights.

NEW YEAR'S EVE is a big night. Like Lexus's "December to Remember", New Year's Eve is a time to put a big red bow on the current year. Or, if your year was a lemon, it's time to put on some Del Amitri and kiss this thing goodbye. Either way, New Year's Eve is the biggest party night of the year because we save the best for last. Or do we always start with a bang? (I always forget.)

With each new year comes new expectations. We set goals and resolutions for the next 365 days. It's exciting to think that, like a new Weight Watchers promotional offer, our new and improved version hits the shelves every January 1st.

Most of us believe our lives, habits, and body mass index will all get better, *starting tomorrow morning*, which makes the new year an exciting time. So here is a simple thing you can do on New Year's Eve to give yourself the best possible start.

I know Ryan Seacrest (RIP Dick Clark) wants you to stay up until midnight to watch the ball drop in Times Square. Don't. Go to bed at a decent hour. Not only is going to sleep early on New Year's Eve a wonderfully rebellious move, but it also sets you up for success.

The first time I went to bed before midnight on New Year's Eve was a couple of years ago. And I loved it.

You don't get any credit or bonus points in the old year or the new one if you stay up to witness the clock tick to midnight. There will be very little productivity between 10pm and midnight. And if you haven't made your goals in the first 364 days and 22 hours of the year, you're not likely to achieve them in the last 120 minutes. (Plus, "Auld Lang Syne" is a pretty dumb song. I presume it is about Mr. Syne, who lived next door to me when I was growing up in Vermont. He wasn't worth singing about at any hour.)

You're not going to get a jumpstart on your goals, hopes, dreams, or resolutions by staying up past midnight on New Year's Eve. You're just going to get tired. And maybe hungover—neither of which (I'm guessing) you really want.

But if you do stay up until midnight on December 31st, one of two things will happen:

1. You won't get an early start on January 1st.

Getting an early start to your day is the best way to be productive. So it follows that if you are motivated to achieve more in the year ahead, you'll want to get up early and get going.

2. You won't get a good night's sleep.

Let's say you stay up late to celebrate NYE, and then you also get up early on January 1st. You will not be fully recharged, fully energized, or fully ready to make January 1st an outstanding start. If you are serious about making positive changes, you should seriously get serious about creating good sleep habits, starting on day one.

As the experts say, aim for getting a good eight hours of sleep every night. New Year's Eve is no different. Try getting to bed by 10:30 pm and waking up by 6:30 am. As we all know, the end is determined by how we begin. One great step leads to another. And one great day leads to another. Remember, the longer you wait to get into a new, positive habit, the less likely it will happen.

LAST BITE

Success goes to bed early and gets up early. Get a great night of sleep. Then, start each day early, well-rested, recharged, and re-energized. It's the best way to make the best day.

CHAPTER 36

Ask For What You Want.

IN 2019 MY family traveled to the Pacific Northwest for our summer vacation. We wanted to see so much that mapping out our route and scheduling our stops over nine days was a challenge, especially because we wanted to visit British Columbia. (Which I would have named Canadian Columbia, but what do I know?)

The thing my son Johann wanted to see most was the Oregon Rail Heritage Museum in Portland. But, unfortunately, the museum's schedule posed a problem. It was only open Thursday through Sunday. And when we finalized the logistics, we would be in Portland on a Tuesday, when the museum was closed.

However, the museum was across the street from another site we planned to hit, the Oregon Museum of Science and Industry.

So my wife Dawn told Johann that we would drive by the train museum and see whatever we could see from the outside.

As we approached the building, we did see a few train engines and train cars outside, which was nice but not enough. Johann was so interested in this museum because it held one of his all-time favorite trains. The magnificent Daylight 4449. The only remaining train of its type. The Daylight was inside, and we could not see it from the outside.

Dawn suggested that we park the car at the closed museum parking lot and look at the closed facility. So we did. In the process, we encountered several signs reminding us that the museum was closed that day. I felt a little silly getting out of the car, like Clark Griswold parking at an obviously closed Wally World.

As we spilled out of the car and made our way to the fence surrounding the museum grounds, Dawn spotted two people who looked like they worked at the museum. They were exiting the closed building, and she was walking briskly toward them. She was in Deion Sanders mode and was trying to intercept them.

I cringed at the idea of what Dawn was going to say to these people. She's aggressive. It's a trait more in sync with her years living in New York City and Chicago than her childhood years in Wausau, Wisconsin.

I kept my distance as I watched Dawn intercept the unassuming man and woman at the gate. I could hear her sweetly explaining that we had come all the way from Wisconsin. And that our son Johann would really, really love to see the Daylight 4449. I braced for the employees to remind her that the museum was closed for cleaning and repairs. And that the sign out front should have told her that.

Instead, the man and woman both smiled at her story. Then, suddenly, the man unlocked the gate and invited us in. Moments later, we were standing inside a large hangar. We were staring straight ahead at the grand prize—the Daylight 4449.

Johann finally got to lay his eyes on the prize, thanks to his mama.

Because the museum was closed, we didn't get the standard view of the train. Instead, the wonderful people of the museum gave us an all-access pass to every part of the train, with the engineer as our personal tour guide. Our whole family got to climb up in the cab, past the "Please Keep Off" signs, which was my favorite part.

Johann got stories and insights that most people would have never heard. We felt like distinguished guests and VIPs at the train museum. It was a very special experience. And all for one simple reason: Dawn asked if we could go inside.

That experience provided everyone in our family with an important life lesson. It taught us that if you want something, you have to put yourself in a position to get it. You have to be willing to ask for what you want and not be afraid to get a "*No*". A closed door will sometimes open for you if you ask. And some of the best experiences are on the other side of a locked door.

It pays to be earnest and honest about how much something means to you and ask for what you want. The worst thing that can happen is you hear "No". And in that case, you are no worse off than you were before. But if you get a "Yes", it could open the doors to incredible new experiences and possibilities.

LAST BITE

A closed-door will open when you show just how much you want to go inside. Remember, someone holds the keys to unlock every locked door.

CHAPTER 37

Why Not You?

DICK ENBERG WAS the television sportscaster of my youth. He was the play-by-play announcer for eight Super Bowls, the Olympics, The Masters, Wimbledon, Major League Baseball, college basketball, and boxing. His catchphrase, "Oh, my!", followed many of the greatest athletic feats I witnessed as a child. It was simple and powerful.

When I was a senior in college, Dick Enberg came to the University of Wisconsin to give a speech at a banquet honoring student-athletes for their high academic performance. I was a discus and hammer thrower on the track team and I was proud to attend the event as one of a dozen student-athletes who had earned a 4.0 GPA the previous semester. But I was even more excited that Dick Enberg was going to be speaking.

Three days before the event, I learned that the athletic department had also arranged a private luncheon at the McClain Athletic Center the day of the banquet. Seventeen student-athletes were invited to have lunch with Mr. Enberg and discuss issues facing student-athletes. I was one of the lucky few who received an invitation.

I arrived early to the luncheon, as the school had requested. The athletic staff gave us the game plan and a reminder that we represented the university and the athletic department. (Which I assumed meant don't talk with your mouth full or burp the alphabet.)

The student-athletes waited with great anticipation for Dick to arrive. Once he had been escorted into the room, there was a brief introduction. Then, an athletic staff member announced, "we will let Mr. Enberg go through the food line first, then the students can follow."

I quickly realized that someone would have to follow Dick. And I thought, "Why not me?"

So this discus thrower from little Norwich, Vermont marched across the room to the banquet table. I grabbed a plate and stepped in line right behind Dick Enberg, one of the greatest sports broadcasters of all time. As we walked through the line, we talked. And when Dick took his seat, I took the seat right next to him. Someone had to. Why not me?

The next hour was amazing. We had a great group conversation. Dick showed a genuine interest in our thoughts and perspectives. I shared the challenges of being an in-season athlete in the spring of my senior year, which made it hard to find time to pursue a job for post-graduation.

Dick wisely predicted that the same level of commitment I brought to my athletic and academic success would translate well to my professional career. He encouraged me to enjoy the rest of my senior year. (Which, of course, I did.)

That evening, I attended the banquet with my favorite journalism professor, Roger Rathke, and my aunt, Deanie Sprau. She lived in Madison and was a huge reason I had chosen The University of Wisconsin. The banquet was at The Great Hall at the Memorial Union. About 500 attendees packed into the huge room, including student-athletes, faculty, staff, and family members. It felt like a large wedding. Our assigned table was at the center of the large banquet hall. Dick Enberg sat at the head table with Athletic Director, Pat Richter and other university dignitaries.

It was fun to see all of the athletes trade in their athletic department sweatpants and t-shirts for dresses and suits. The room was buzzing. Everyone was excited to have one of America's best-known sports figures in attendance. And the student-athletes were pumped about the free meal.

After a warm welcome to the event by the master of ceremonies, we began the meal. In the middle of the evening, Dick stood up and started making his way across the large, packed hall. I presumed he was either going to visit the little broadcasters' room or step out for a moment to review his notes one last time before his speech.

All eyes were on Mr. Enberg as he cut across the middle of the vast ballroom. I quickly recognized that he was on a path that would take him directly past my table. He got closer and closer to me. When he reached my table, he paused for a brief moment, he gave me a big smile, and patted me on the back like we were old friends. Then he continued on his way and disappeared from the room.

Immediately, friends flocked to my table to find out why, in this room of 500 people, had the guest of honor stopped to say hi to some random (albeit studious) track athlete. My answer was as simple as it was smug. I said, *"Oh, we had lunch together today."*

The rest of the event was nice. Dick gave another great speech, and I was proud to be part of this large group of high-achieving intercollegiate student-athletes. But more importantly, the evening serves as a shining reminder of how life works. Your efforts can get you into the room. But then, the relationships you develop along the way are what make you stand out from the crowd.

Dick Enberg was right about my career, too. After I graduated, my professor Roger Rathke, who was with me at the banquet that night, introduced me to his college buddy, Paul Counsell. At the time, Paul was the CEO of the remarkable advertising agency Cramer Krasselt. Paul granted me an informational interview and then offered me a job as a copywriter. And today, I own an agency where I get to employ others.

Thank you, Dick Enberg. For the Super Bowls, the Olympics, and mostly for coming to Madison and having lunch and dinner with me. Thank you for the opportunity to discover what can happen when you adopt a why-not-me attitude. And thank you for the wise career advice. Things have worked out fine. Just like you said they would.

LAST BITE

If not you, then who? Even though your efforts are needed to get you in the room, it's your relationships that turn the room into a launchpad.

CHAPTER 38

Always Bet On Yourself.

CHANCES ARE, BY now, you know that you didn't win last week's Powerball lottery jackpot. (Sorry.) And if you are like most Americans who played, you were probably off by five or six numbers. I know how you feel because when I was 18, I had a lottery experience that forever shaped my perspective on this game that promises the chance of instant riches.

It happened at my high school graduation. My classmates and I received our Hanover High School diplomas from our principal, the late, super great Uwe Bagnato. As he handed us our diplomas, we each handed him a lottery ticket.

It was an exciting experiment. We all wondered how much Groovy Uwe might win with 150 chances. (In case you think that's a small high school class, you should know that we scoured ten towns from two states to come up with 150 educable kids.)

We imagined Uwe would become mega-rich, and we would be the last class to graduate under his 'principality'. But when we discovered that he only won a couple of bucks and would be back at work again after Labor Day, the lottery was forever dead to me.

It was then that I officially decided it would be better to bet on myself instead. I have made my career as an advertising creative. As a professional creative thinker, I make my money through the ideation lottery. In this game, the ideas bounce around in your head like lottery balls, randomized for fairness. And when your mental machinery cues those idea-balls to drop into your consciousness, you either have winning ideas or losing ideas.

I love the odds in this game. I stack them in my favor by absorbing the world around me through interesting experiences, reading, human interactions, and sweet tea.

What I like even better is that you can play the idea lottery non-stop. And I do. For some, it is nerve-racking to make your living in this manner. That's why so many creative thinkers burn out or switch professions. But the ones who stick with it are often well rewarded.

The value of the creative lottery is summed up beautifully in one of my favorite quotes:

"More gold had been mined from the mind of men than the earth itself."
— Napoleon Hill, *Think and Grow Rich*

Hill wrote powerful ideas about the minds of men. But the idea of ideas is strange. I have no idea where the ideas really come from. Sure, sometimes the thoughts are mashups of two things I've considered recently. And sometimes, there is a strong logic chain that leads me to an idea. But a healthy percentage of the time, God just drops gold nuggets in between my ears, and for all I know, I have nothing to do with it. I'm just smart enough to watch for them, recognize them when I see them, and polish them enough to enable others to realize their value.

The next time you watch those lottery balls mixing, think of them like the creative ideas that have formed in the minds of men and women and turned those individuals into millionaires and billionaires. I hope it encourages you to bet on your ideas instead. And take it from me, Principal Uwe Bagnato and the Hanover High School class of 1991, the chances of winning the lottery are far better in your head.

LAST BITE

Always bet on yourself. Bet on your ideas. Bet on your intuition. Bet on your determination. And on your willingness to affect the outcome. Stack the odds in your favor. It is the best way to mitigate risk and set yourself up for an epic payout.

CHAPTER 39

Don't Build A Network.
Build Friendships.

WHEN I WAS in college, I started hearing career-minded folks talk about a magical activity called networking. Professors, advisors, and guest speakers discussed networking as if it was the key to success. I had never heard of networking, and I seemed to have gotten along just fine, but what did I know?

When I started my career in advertising, I heard even more about the practice of networking. Business books and career coaches prescribe networking like business vitamins to help boost your career health. Nevertheless, I still didn't fully understand what networking was or why everyone was talking about it.

So what does it mean to network? To figure it out, I started with a simple step. I looked up the definition in the dictionary. Here's what I found:

"Network (verb): Interact with other people to exchange information and develop contacts, especially to further one's career."

Okay, that's clear. I understood what networking meant. And it made me want to barf. Because "interacting with people", "exchanging information" and "developing contacts" are things that can be done by a machine. Or a criminal. Where's the talent or value?

Other people may choose to network, but I don't. I continue to do what I did before college and before people tried to convince me that networking was the secret to career advancement and successful entrepreneurship.

I don't network. I befriend.

What does that mean? Well, I just happen to have the definition for you right here:

"Befriend (verb): Act as a friend to someone by offering help or support."

This is what I do. I learned how to do this when I was in preschool and it has served me well my entire life. Notice the keys to befriending? "Act as a friend" and "offer help and support". These are personal. This is the good stuff. It's what other people really want. And it's how you improve life on this big blue marble.

When you dive into the following synonyms of befriending, you develop an even richer picture:

- ▶ Make friends with
- ▶ Make a friend of

- ► Look after
- ► Keep an eye on
- ► Be of service to
- ► Lend a helping hand to
- ► Help
- ► Protect
- ► Side with
- ► Stand by
- ► Encourage

Your relationships and the positive impact you have on others are the only things that actually matter. It is true at home. It is true in preschool. It is true in college. And it is true in business. So if you want to be a great success make a lot of great friends.

LAST BITE

Prioritize developing genuine relationships. Because when you make people the most important thing in your life, everything else magically falls into place.

CHAPTER 40

I LIKE INVESTING. I started investing in stocks not long after landing my first job after college. Back then, I didn't really know what I was doing. I made mistakes, but I wasn't afraid. I kept reading, listening, and studying investment strategies. Today, I have a solid, repeatable approach. That's because I stole my strategy from Warren Buffett, who stole his strategy from Benjamin Graham, the Babe Ruth of value investing.

I bought Graham's book, *The Intelligent Investor*, because I heard it was the bible on stock investing. The 600-page book boils down to this one idea: Buy when a stock is undervalued. Sell when it is overvalued.

This strategy has served me well. I'm always looking to get in on a good company's bad news. So when banks were collapsing because of the mortgage crisis, I bought Huntington, Fifth Third, and PNC stock. When there was oil gushing in the Gulf of Mexico, I bought BP. When Equifax was hacked, I was into Equifax stock. When diseases were decimating the US chicken population, I shouted, "Pass me a drumstick and some shares of Pilgrim's Pride and Sanderson Farms!"

Then came the COVID-19 crisis, and I invested more than ever. I bought more shares in banks and even more shares in oil companies. I bought Disney when the stock was on Crash Mountain because of theme park closures, cruise stoppages, and a halt of live sports.

I invest in people the same way I invest in stocks. When people are hot, have the world by the bizzles, and everyone wants to be close to them, they don't need my help. I like to invest in people who have lost their jobs, hit icebergs, or are leaking oil. Those are the people who need an infusion of confidence and friendship. It is easy to divest when people hit all-time lows. But that's when I like to double down.

People always rebound. Your personal stock always rises again to reflect your actual value. So when you pick someone up who feels like they are sitting on the discard pile, the return you get for your invested time and attention truly appreciates. You know that things will get better for that person even when they can't see it. Because when you feel like you are swirling around the toilet, it is hard to see past the closing lid.

LAST BITE

Look for ways to invest in those who need it most; the good people, organizations, and teams that have fallen out of favor. Because the belief, support, and confidence you invest in them will buoy you both in amazing ways.

CHAPTER 41

Become A Better Listener.

I WORK IN advertising so I know the value of the "new and improved". That is why I am always trying to create a newer, more improved version of myself. At the beginning of my career, I recognized that I would have to do my homework if I wanted to catch up to the best professionals in this industry. So I began studying and learning. Not in a structured school program, but in a self-directed, choose-your-own-adventure, movie montage kind of way.

Like most people who are into self-improvement, I have focused heavily on refining my public speaking, pitch presenting, and salesmanship skills. The deeper I get into this game that Prince called "*life*", I realize that most people (including me) spend too much time on the wrong side of the equation.

The most effective and important communication skill is knowing when *not* to speak.

Listening is where all success starts. It is only through listening that we understand the problems that we need to solve. It is how we hear what *isn't* said. (Don't think too hard about this concept, or it sounds really stupid).

Through listening, we learn about other people. We learn about their history, their values, styles, and quirks. And what we learn allows for deeper, more meaningful, and more valuable relationships.

When was the last time you heard about someone going to a listening seminar? Unlike public speaking and sales, the listening industry is not saturated with options for self-improvement. So if you are looking for your next great opportunity, maybe you should think about the listening space. It could quietly become the next big thing. Even bigger than plastics. Until then, here are some ideas that are sure to make you a better, bigger-eared version of yourself.

Six Ways to Improve Your Listening Skills:

1. Listen Competitively

Start by trying to be really good at listening. You already know the little things you have to do to be a great listener. We learned them by playing Simon Says. Look at the person talking. Give the speaker your full attention. Do it like your earning potential, relationships, and *Parent of the Year* award depend on it. They do.

2. Shut Your Mouth

We are often so compelled to talk that we stop listening. If you want to be a great listener, you have to silence your impulses and focus on your role as a listener. Doing this means you are not providing answers, solutions, or opinions. You are harvesting, not planting. Know what season it is. Bring the right equipment to the field.

3. Keep Your Partner Lubricated

I don't mean with alcohol or KY. With affirmations and demonstrated interest. Lean in. Show you care. And you will keep others pouring out their thoughts, feelings, and information.

4. Listen With Your Spidey Senses

Hear beyond the words that are said. Note the tone and emotion. Those things are like limps, signaling that something deeper is wrong. Or they could signal that someone is in a good mood that exceeds the norm for the current situation. Maybe they just got engaged. Or perhaps they are on drugs.

5. Playback, Jack

The curtain call of any good listening session is the summary of what you heard. Repeat back to them the highlighted, simplified summary that demonstrates that you really heard and value their thoughts. Do this and you will always leave a conversation with more personal equity.

6. Lock Up the Valuables

One of the most essential listening skills is keeping the private stuff private. You have to know which things you heard that were intended for you alone, and not talk about them. When people believe that you are trustworthy, they tell you more. You become a confidante and an insider. It's like being sponge-worthy.

LAST BITE

Listening skills represent the greatest untapped potential for most humans. Tap into better listening skills today, and they will provide you with an advantage for the rest of your life. You'll enjoy better relationships with your friends, family, and co-workers. Better solutions to problems. More and better networking. And better creative ideas.

CHAPTER 42

Put The Results In Their Hands.

WHEN I FIRST became a parent I was prepared to drop knowledge on my kids. I had prepared a syllabus of over 30 years worth of life lessons. They were sorted into two files. The first was labeled "Smart Things I Did". The second was labeled "Dumb Things I Did That You Should Avoid".

What I wasn't prepared for were all of the lessons that my children would teach me. My latest lessons have come from my 11-year-old son Magnus. He has taught me a lot about socializing. He has a remarkable ability to make instantaneous friendships anywhere. His social intelligence is as good as some of the best adults I know. He's like a little Dale Carnegie on the playground, just winning little friends and influencing little people.

But as impressive as Magnus is at socializing, he is world-class at losing teeth. It's an odd thing to be great at, I know. But for a time, Magnus was losing teeth faster than a meth addict. At one point, he lost eight teeth in two months. In fact, I don't know how he was able to chew food for a while.

However, it is not the amount of teeth lost that impresses me, it is the style in which he loses them. You know how I know when Magnus has a loose tooth? He puts the tooth in my hand. He doesn't talk about it, complain about it or brag about it. He says nothing until the tooth is out. Even then he doesn't really talk about it. He just shows me the results, and grins with an even gappier smile. Every time he surprises me (and the Tooth Fairy) with no advanced warning, I am more impressed by his ability to quietly take care of his business.

I meet people all the time who go on and on, (like Steven Bishop, down in Jamaica, with lots of pretty women), about their big dreams, lofty goals and ambitious plans. But talk doesn't bring a dream to life. Discussions don't achieve goals. And ambition doesn't execute a plan. Talk is the cheapest of all commodities. Action is the most valuable. And it is the only currency you can use to buy your goals and dreams.

LAST BITE

Success requires action. To be successful, do more. Talk less. Complain less. Analyze less. And focus on results. Don't tell the world what you are going to do. Show them what you've done. Then, after the work is all done, you can sit back and enjoy the rewards. Just like my son Magnus does.

CHAPTER 43

Read To Learn. Then Act.

I LOVE TO READ. Like most people, I was born highly uneducated. Reading has become an instrumental part of my plan to overcome my early shortcomings. I love to learn and to become inspired. And if you are reading this, I expect you do, too.

I like reading classic literature because it makes me feel worldly. At one point, I enjoyed reading the first three Harry Potter books because they made me feel magical. But then I realized my life was too short to read four more books about a fanciful wizard boy. I read many biographies and books on self-improvement and business. I also read healthy portions of magazines like *Fast Company* and *Inc.* because I find them both creatively stimulating and educational. And I like the pictures.

Several years ago, I read an interesting quote from Charlie "Tremendous" Jones that said,

"You are the same today as you'll be in five years except for two things: the books you read and the people you meet."
— Charlie "Tremendous" Jones, *Life is Tremendous*

This quote about reading encouraged Adam "Ordinary" Albrecht to read even more. But I don't read too much. That's because I have found that too much reading leads to too little doing. If you fill all your time with learning and inspiration, you leave no time for action.

When I began my entrepreneurial journey, I created a simple rule that has influenced my reading ever since.

Read just enough to learn something new and become inspired. Then act on it.

By following this rule, I have accomplished more. I've wasted less time. And I'm more excited about my work.

Today, I think of reading like a pre-game speech that I listen to just long enough to become properly motivated. And as soon as I am revved up, I jump to work, acting on the inspiration.

That's when I start writing, planning, structuring, detailing, calling, creating, wizarding, or potioning. And what I've found is that when I have one hour available, I can read for 10-15 minutes and then I can spend the rest of the hour acting on what I have learned. And the return on that one hour is significantly higher.

LAST BITE

Read enough each day to want to do something new and exciting. Then do it. Repeat.

CHAPTER 44

Arrive Smarter Than You Left.

IF YOU ARE not actively learning every day, you are in danger of slipping into a long intellectual decline. It is easy to absorb all kinds of knowledge in school, but once we leave high school or college (or become a *beauty school dropout*), we have to actively seek ways to keep learning. (Okay, okay, maybe we still learn something new every day by picking up trivia under a Snapple cap. For example, did you know that the first touch-tone phones didn't have pound or star symbols, or that Americans invented what we thought was authentic Mexican, Italian, and Chinese food? Interesting, but it's not exactly growth-learning.)

Actual growth learning is extremely important to me. I learned at an early age that the stock version of myself was pretty ordinary. I have a vision of myself as a much better, smarter, stronger, funnier, nicer, braver, more capable human than I am today. It's why I always try to close the gap between the *me* in my head and the *me* on my couch.

One of the best habits I have developed to create a better me is listening to audiobooks while I drive. I stumbled onto my audiobook interest accidentally. In 2009, I attended the Hachette Book Group's annual book sale just north of Indianapolis. For one weekend in June, everything is on sale for just one dollar. So I bet one dollar on Ted Turner's *Call Me Ted* audiobook. I loved the book and more importantly, I learned from it.

1. I learned how a kid who didn't apply himself well in school could become one of the world's wealthiest people by applying himself well in life.
2. I learned that to make wild leaps in your accomplishments, you sometimes need to take wild risks.
3. I learned that meeting room antics can make you highly memorable.
4. I learned that pursuing your passionate interests can change the world.
5. I learned that through mergers and acquisitions, you can get tossed out of your own company.
6. I learned the immense impact of philanthropy.
7. I learned the value of keeping your eye on the future.
8. I learned that the first Ted's Montana Grill was in my former hometown of Columbus, Ohio. (To be fair, this tidbit is a little more Snapple cap-esque, but it is interesting to me.)

9. I learned how the right people and processes could turn a last place team like the Atlanta Braves into World Series Champions.
10. I learned that Jane Fonda is a pretty great lady to have on your arm when you walk into a party.

I enjoyed *Call Me Ted* so much that I sought out more audiobooks. I listened to biographies and self-help books. I listened to history books and books about the future. Now I pick up nuggets of knowledge and pearls of wisdom every day when I drive. I will often stop the audiobook and ask Siri to take notes, record quotes, or record me paraphrasing a lesson for review later. It's my way of highlighting important passages as I listen, just like I did in college, except hands-free and with my eyes on the road.

It didn't take long for the audiobooks to make me feel like I was winning at life. By listening to and learning from books on my commute, I would arrive at work smarter than when I left the house. And then, later that day, I would arrive home even smarter than I was when I left the office.

Since leaving college, no activity has added so many layers of depth to my thinking, new lenses through which to view the world, or examples for how to choose my adventures like my audiobook lessons. Today, my agency owns a library of audiobook titles that our team can check out anytime they want. It's the easiest way I know of to grow a stronger and smarter team without adding new people.

I encourage you to stop by your local library to check out the audiobook section before your next road trip, flight, or commute.

I bet you'll be surprised by the range of titles and topics. And it's all free (unless you count the taxes you already paid that bought the books).

There are also plenty of digital resources, like Audible and Amazon, which offer almost any book title you can imagine. And when you find a title you like, shoot me a message. I am always looking for a great new listen.

LAST BITE

Your commute is one of the best opportunities for self-improvement. Listen to audiobooks or podcasts. Learn, grow and take advantage of your time. Invest in yourself as you drive. You will always arrive at your destination as a more enriched person.

CHAPTER 45

I BET YOU have good ideas all the time. I bet you have ideas about inventions you should create, businesses you should start, books you should write, and funny comebacks you should have said. Just like George Costanza's Jerk Store.

We all dream of writing a bestseller or starting a business that could grace the cover of *Forbes* magazine. For most people, these are never more than dreams. That's because, unfortunately, most people have no idea how easy it is to make their dreams a reality.

One simple element changes dreamers into doers. Action. To make a dream come true, you simply need to step towards it. You don't need a giant Giannis Antetokounmpo-sized step. Any baby step will do.

When I really wanted to start my advertising agency, I started taking little actions that moved the idea forward. First, I bought and read books about starting and running a business. I followed the advice in the books and wrote down my plans. Then I started following them. I met with entrepreneurs and gleaned their insights and advice.

None of it was hard. Within months, I had started a business in my spare time that would support my family. A business that ultimately may create significant wealth. All because I kept taking baby steps.

Recently I have taken small but meaningful steps forward on several new projects:

1. I created a growing monthly meetup with my college track and field teammates that I think could have a major impact on many lives.
2. I started writing a script for a live show that I think could become a template for live entertainment shows in every city in the world.
3. I took steps forward to create a new food brand because I recognized an opportunity no one else was grabbing.
4. I contacted a publication and told them I was interested in writing a regular segment for them. I now have a meeting with the publishers.
5. I started writing two books.
6. I have actively studied real estate investing and have been looking at properties to buy.
7. I have sketched ideas for new t-shirts I want to create.

I am thrilled to have started all of these projects. But they are not a reality yet. They all require more action. In fact, none of the eight things I started can or will move forward without me. So the baby steps have to continue. But if I keep moving, I will have a new line of t-shirts to wear and sell, a food brand you could find at grocery stores, a real estate business, two books, a meetup group format that could be repeated around the world, a regular column in a publication, and a crazy live show you would pay money to see (even though everyone in the show wears clothes).

When you get an inkling that you should create or do something, take baby steps towards it. It's how I created my agency. And it is how I'll be able to bring all of my other ideas to life, too.

LAST BITE

Action is everything. It is the difference between dreams that come true and those that vanish into the ether. Talk is cheap. Action is magic. If you just keep taking baby steps, you will have completed a marathon of progress before you know it.

CHAPTER 46

Start Slower To Go Farther.

I ALWAYS FIND the beginning of the year odd. It kicks off with resolution season, the magical four-week period when everyone wants to change their lives for the better. For regular gym-goers, it is the worst time of year. You arrive for your regular workout only to find some dude who hasn't exercised in eleven months, wheezing and dripping all over your treadmill.

You probably have a list of things you want to start, stop, or improve. I applaud that. But far too often, we fail to turn our resolutions into powerful new habits. So I will share my secret, counterintuitive technique that makes creating a healthy new pattern much easier.

It is natural to assume that if you want to make a major change in your life, you should work hard at it. That approach works for some. The beaver loves to be busy. The sled dog loves to mush. The couch potato loves to *potate* on the couch. But, unfortunately, hard work simply reminds most people how much they dislike hard work. That's why the activity fails to develop into a habit.

There is a simpler approach. My secret formula for goal achievement is to put in less effort. While it is natural to think that hard work in the gym or the office will get you better results faster, it actually can hamper your long-term success. Most people quickly grow tired of the work, the suffering, the pain, and the sacrifice.

I recommend getting lazy to get ahead. When I start a new habit or resume my workout routine after a pause, I do less than I could. I do less than I should. And that is the key. By under exerting myself, I keep the activity enjoyable. I check the box. I worked out or spent time on the project or studied, or whatever the case may be, but I only did the minimum. Or the medium. But never even close to the maximum. At first.

Doing Less Does Three Things For You:

1. It makes you feel accomplished.

After all, you did work towards your goal. You got on the cardio machine. You lifted weights. You created an initial sketch of the business you wanted to start. You skipped dessert. (Yay you! You're doing it!)

2. It makes it fun.
You did the parts that make the endeavor enjoyable. You worked up some sweat. But you didn't push hard enough to suffer. You didn't cramp. You didn't feel like throwing up. You didn't overload your brain. And most importantly, you never wished that it was over.

3. It makes you hungry for more.
This is the key. You finish knowing you can do more. You know you have more in you, even in this early stage so you look forward to more.

Hard work requires calluses. You need to build up your layers of armor. You do this through repetition. Slowly, repeatedly over time. Your body develops a tolerance to work and motion so you can withstand more.

The problem is that most people blister. They work harder than they are prepared for in the beginning. And their body or brain rejects the work. The effort feels more like a threat than a treat. You get sore, and the pain says stop. The skin bubbles and peels off, and then you bleed. All the feedback is negative. The rational person rejects the activity and retreats to the couch to *potate*.

But people who slowly build calluses keep going. They see the improvement they are after. Which means they can increase the effort without decreasing the fun. They feel accomplished and prepared for more. It's a beautiful thing.

When I started The Weaponry, I had a vision for the perfect, fully-formed agency. And I started small. And slow. I didn't worry about everything I should be doing or that I would eventually need to do to make the business in my head a reality. If I tried to do it all from the beginning, I would have likely been overwhelmed, stressed, or scared. Instead, I did a little bit more every day. And it's been fun the entire time. The kind of fun that keeps me coming back for more.

LAST BITE

Don't go crazy right out of the gate. Underdo it. Make it fun. And make yourself want to come back for more– plan for long-term success. But allow yourself time to build momentum. By doing so, you can change your life forever.

CHAPTER 47

Today's Success Was Born Yesterday.

TIME IS THE world's most precious resource. That's why great success requires great time management. I'd argue that knowing how to properly budget and invest your time is even more important to your ultimate success than budgeting and investing your money.

When I began planning to launch The Weaponry, there was a tremendous amount of work to be done. I knew the way I invested my time during that first year would determine the fate of my startup. As I neared the end of each workweek, I noticed something interesting about my progress. I repeatedly saw how the activities on one particular day were making all the difference.

There are at least seven different opinions as to which day is the most important. Elton John thinks it is Saturday. Mick

Jagger claims it's Tuesday. The Mamas and Papas all say Monday (repeatedly). However, five years into my entrepreneurial journey, I know Paul McCartney was right. I can confidently state that the most critical day for achieving great things is yesterday.

All of your success comes from what you did yesterday. The relationships you developed yesterday strengthen your support system today. The progress you made yesterday becomes momentum today. The exercise you performed yesterday creates today's strength, endurance, and health. The time you invested yesterday becomes the time you saved today.

The reading you did yesterday creates the knowledge you have today. The traveling you did yesterday becomes today's memories and experiences. Your preparation yesterday makes you ready today.

As a business owner, I know that today's workload comes from yesterday's business development efforts. As a professional ideator, I know that my creativity springs from what I absorbed yesterday. As a capable human, I know that my confidence grows based on the successes and the failures I experienced yesterday. And the eviction notice I didn't get comes from the rent I paid yesterday.

I am always grateful for the activities I had the foresight and energy to do yesterday. The workout I completed. The process I created. The book I read. The research I performed and the relationship I fostered. In the moment, procrastination often feels like the easier route. This is why it is so valuable to view the moment as if it were yesterday.

There is a great Chinese proverb I think about often.

"The best time to plant a tree was 20 years ago. The second best time is right now."

The truth is, in less than 24 hours, today will be yesterday. And when the clock strikes midnight, you will be either smarter, stronger, and more prepared, or you will be in the same position you are in today.

Big success is a result of the accumulation of small actions. The To-Do list you complete today will become tomorrow's momentum. That momentum will help you power past barriers that would have previously stopped you.

LAST BITE

Today will soon be gone. Tomorrow is a mystery. But yesterday is your library, your museum, your toolbox, and your bonding agent. Yesterday puts wind in your sails. And the winds of yesterday determine both the direction and the speed at which you travel today.

CHAPTER 48

DURING A CAR ride a couple of years ago, I heard my children debating a topic in the back seat. At one point, my then thirteen-year-old daughter Ava argued an important precedent that she felt had been set the day before. My son Johann had this simple and elegant response:

"Today is not yesterday."
— Johann Albrecht (11 y/o)

I love this declaration. It serves as both an inspiration and a warning. Indeed, today is not yesterday. If you had a bad day yesterday, forget about it. It's over. Today you get to start fresh. Today is a chance to bounce back. It's a whole new chance to be great. To be productive and smart. To be the you that you want to be.

If you had a great day yesterday, full of success, productivity, and Maslow-quality self-actualization, remember that yesterday is gone with the wind. Today, you may have to begin again. To capitalize on a great yesterday and build momentum, you need to put in the work again today.

LAST BITE

Always remember that you are either getting better or you are getting worse. You get to decide which direction you are going every single day. Make the most of it. It's the least you can do.

CHAPTER 49

Build Your Ark Under Blue Skies.

HIGH ACHIEVERS CONSTANTLY talk about the importance of hard work. But hard work is hard to define. That's because what is hard for one person is easy for another. We each define hard work based on our capacity for struggle and our tolerance for strain. Still, it is helpful to have a universal way to think about hard work. (Even if you only plan to think about it in a small corner of the universe.)

I turn to the pastor, author, and leadership leader John C. Maxwell for insight into hard work. This is what my man JCM has to say on the subject:

> "Hard work is the accumulation of easy things you didn't do when you should have."

I like Maxwell's definition. But I have modified it for my own purposes. I say:

"Hard work is the easy work you didn't do when you had more time."

The critical element that makes hard work hard is the time constraint, which means that hard work has to do with work density. Written pseudo-mathematically:

Difficulty of Work = Amount of Work ÷ Time To Do It

According to this formula, if you start your work earlier and spread it over more time, it makes it easier. You feel the burden of work when you have to exert a high level of effort over a short amount of time. The formula works for any type of work. Start working on that next big project now. Start studying earlier for the exam. Clean a little every day, and it won't feel like a colossal undertaking.

Since launching my agency, I have been pleasantly surprised by how many times something was easier because I unwittingly did the work ahead of time. I spent the last several decades doing the hard work of entrepreneurship, well before I decided to become an entrepreneur. I did this by developing relationships, building trust, demonstrating real interest, and connecting dots.

LAST BITE

If you want to achieve great things, be proactive. Spend as much time on the important tasks as possible before they become urgent. The easiest way to build an ark is under blue skies. Eventually, it will rain. And when it does, you'll be happy you gave yourself a head start. Just ask Noah.

CHAPTER 50

Your Critical Electives Matter Most.

I LOVED MY college experience, but when I graduated, I was as thrilled to be done with school as Alice Cooper. I didn't realize then that I was far from done with my education. Since I graduated from the University of Wisconsin, I have been busy acquiring self-directed micro-degrees.

How? By reading. And not just reading for reading's sake. I am constantly seeking out new books, magazines, and articles to help me become a smarter, more effective human, a better business person, and a more creative thinker.

One of my favorite micro-degrees came from reading Stephen R. Covey's classic, *The 7 Habits of Highly Effective People.* Reading books like these is akin to taking a college course, only without the chance to meet an attractive co-ed. I have learned, retained, and applied more from books like these than from many of my college courses. (Sorry not sorry to the professor who taught my Psychology of Emotions class junior year. That was worthless.)

In his best-selling book, Covey introduces a concept that I absolutely love. It's the idea of spending more time doing things that are important but not urgent. I call these the "pivotal electives", and they're the source of magic in your life. When I learned about this concept, I realized that I had already done a lot of work in this quadrant.

Nurturing these pivotal electives has been a fundamental reason for all of the good things that have happened in my career. As I continue growing my business, this type of activity is even more crucial.

As part of my pivotal electives, I seek talented people to join our team, and I begin planting seeds. I plant seeds all the time that I don't expect to bear fruit, nuts, or vegetables for years. There are talented people across America who I have been talking to about joining The Weaponry, not in the coming weeks or months, but years from now. Why? Because great things often take a long time to develop. So I want to start the process as early as possible. My goal is not simply to appear on the radar of talented people, but to steer the course of their journey in my direction.

I want to create a gravitational pull towards my organization and me. Through our early conversations, these valued potential recruits can begin imagining us making magic together. By creating an attractive vision of the future, the people start steering their courses towards this attractive future reality.

This early recruiting activity works just like marketing and advertising. Because advertising, through brand awareness and brand affinity, begins to create a gravitational pull towards products and services.

I have spent my entire career planting seeds about the merits of various brands. Eventually, by sharing those merits, customers, clients, and members find their way to the brands that can help solve their problems or enrich their lives. And everyone wins. This is what I am doing now, both personally and professionally. And you can, too.

LAST BITE

To attract the people you want to surround yourself with, start early. Start recruiting well before you need them. Offer a picture of what a friendship, career, or success could look like when you join forces. Do the necessary work early, before it becomes urgent. Then watch as their paths turn in your direction. It's a pretty amazing thing to see. It's what highly effective people do. You know. People like you.

CHAPTER 51

Success Is Mapped Out Day By Day.

MY DAUGHTER AVA has wanted to work at The Weaponry since she was twelve. While a twelve-year-old may not seem like a valuable asset to an ad agency, she is a great writer and a very creative thinker. She created a blog, adapted a novel into a screenplay, and wrote a murder mystery novel. Oh, and she has created a series for IGTV. (But she rarely makes her bed. So maybe she's not *quite* perfect yet.)

She recently asked when she could come to work with me and help out. I told her that I would have to check my schedule to see what might work. She responded with the very simple but surprisingly profound question, " How do you determine your schedule?"

Ava's question made me think more deeply about my schedule. I explained that my schedule starts as a blank slate. To fill it, I start with deadlines. I look at all of the things that the company has to create and the due dates for each. Then I schedule my time to focus on those projects, in order of priority, from hottest to coolest.

But this begs the question of what your schedule would look like if it weren't for deadlines or due dates. For entrepreneurs, there is always something more to do. Isn't this true of every job? How does anyone add tasks to their schedule that don't have deadlines?

There are three recurring activities that I incorporate into my schedule.

Connecting: I am a natural connector. I think people are the most interesting machines on the planet. I highly value my relationships. More importantly, I maintain them. And when I think of someone or have a little bell that dings in the back of my head that lets me know it has been too long since we've last spoken, I reach out.

Closing gaps: At The Weaponry, we explore the gaps between where our organization is today and our ideal, fully-formed organization of the future. As a result, we often think about our shortcomings. (I don't think of them as shortcomings. I simply see things that we are not doing, or don't have yet, that we will in our ideal state.) This activity is about improving our processes, procedures, systems, and infrastructure. Entrepreneurs call this "working on your business". But I think everyone can benefit from more gap closing. (Except maybe The Gap.)

Things that excite me: I always leave room for things that interest me. Since we are an idea generating machine, there are always exciting ideas bouncing around our office. I try to find as much time to explore those ideas as possible. For example, I might consider new ways to look at our clients' challenges. It could be a new product idea, an additional service, or an idea that could transform our business. I often get excited about new ideas for t-shirts, buttons, stickers, and hats for The Weaponry. I love thinking about new messaging for our walls, too. Most businesses could benefit from more time exploring good ideas. I do it every day. Pencil in some time for things that excite you this week.

These activities are important to my regular schedule and they should be part of yours, too.

Whether you use the same method I do, or have your own formula, make sure your daily schedule isn't driven only by email requests and meetings. As Steven R. Covey teaches us in *The 7 Habits of Highly Effective People*, engaging in important, non-urgent activities is a key determinant of long term success.

LAST BITE

Your life is full of deadline-driven must-do's. They become the studs around which you build your daily schedule. But the key to making each day great is the elective activities you work into your calendar.

CHAPTER 52

THIS PLANET IS home to a lot of people. The last time I lined everybody up and counted, I tallied 7.4 billion humans. With that many people, all connected by the interwebs, you have myriad options if you need someone. So whether you need a spouse, an employee, or a plumber, the enormity of the human supply works in your favor.

But we often find ourselves on the other side of the equation. We want to be employed. We want someone to ask us on a date. We want to be hired to snake someone's drain. So how do we stand out in this 7.4 billion person crowd? Management expert Peter Drucker offers this succinct answer to that important question:

"Something special must leave the room when you leave the room."
— Peter Drucker, *The Effective Executive*

Read that again a couple of times. I'll wait.

Do you bring something special everywhere you go? You may have never thought about *yourself* in these terms. If you haven't, you should. Go ahead. I'll wait.

Think about what *you* bring to a room when *you* walk in. What do you add to the meeting, to the organization, to the relationship, to the overall value equation that others do not? What disappears when *you* leave? If you can't come up with anything, you are a *commodity*. Our country places a very specific value on the 'commodity human.' It's called minimum wage.

We have all sat in meetings where there were too many attendees. You can always spot the extraneous attendees because the meeting would have been no different without them. But, on the other hand, you have been in meetings when you asked, "Why are we meeting if Fill-In-The-Name isn't here?" You, my friend, want to be Fill-In-The-Name!

So what leaves the room when you do? Here is a sample of things you might bring to a room. Mix and match to create unique combinations. Or collect them all!

- Energy
- Experience
- Connective tissue
- Humor
- Creativity
- Compassion
- Insight
- Reason

- ▶ Balance
- ▶ Knowledge
- ▶ Relationships
- ▶ Trust
- ▶ Positivity
- ▶ Diversity
- ▶ Know-how
- ▶ Spunk
- ▶ Confidence
- ▶ Reality
- ▶ The wi-fi password

The same principle of specialness that we apply to products and services works as you think about differentiating and marketing yourself. It's like acknowledging what changes if your iPhone breaks, or you lose your Yeti tumbler, or somebody grills generic hotdogs instead of Johnsonville Brats at the backyard party. You can't replace the special, standout options with generic commodities without feeling you have lost something.

You and I both know *you* are not a commodity. Make sure other people recognize the specialness you bring. Reflect on your brand. What are the features and benefits that make you distinct? Identify them. You can use the list as a starting point! Then enhance and augment them so they can't be ignored.

I never want to attend a meeting that I'm not in. Sounds like something Yogi Berra might say, am I right? It's a reason why I make an effort to make even the most boring meetings interesting. It is how I survive them and make them fun for myself. If I continually bring enough to the party that others are disappointed by my absences, we're talking pure Drucker.

LAST BITE

Study your business and social situations. What could you add so that others miss you when you're gone?

CHAPTER 53

Dream It Up. Write It Down. Build It Out.

DO YOU HAVE dreams? I do. (You could say I'm dreamy.) I dream all the time, and I wish more people did. But I also know how to bring my dreams to life. I don't just blow out my birthday candles or wish upon stars or listen to Hall & Oates. While all of those activities may help, I use a simple technique that has proven effective thousands of times.

You may ask yourself how a guy who works in advertising would know how to make dreams come true. Well, my job as a creative is to dream of new things and then bring them to life. My proven system, the "Adam Albrecht approach to creating things" (I just made that up) uses a simple three step process that applies to anything you want to create. A commercial. A home.

A business. An invention. A baby. Or even a commercial about a home business that invents babies.

In my effort to make the world a better place by helping you make more of your dreams come true, I'm sharing this super simple process. Without further ado, here is how you can create anything you want through Adam Albrecht's 3 steps of non-religious creation *(I just rebranded it)*.

Step 1. Envision the dream.

This step is as simple as it sounds. Let your brain run and play. Build castles in your head. This first step is all about dreaming up the perfect fill-in-the-blank (cookie, car wash, app, whatever). Picture the ideal image of it in your head, in HD if it's available in your area. The more detail, the better. This should be fun. Remember to dream big.

Step 2. Write it down.

Again, this is about as simple as it sounds. Even still, 99% of dreams, ideas, and visions never make it to this step. The dreamer fails to write the vision down or describe it. And the dream never takes form.

Simply talking about your dream doesn't cut it. Talking is like dreaming aloud. It's stuck in Step 1. To make your dreams come true, you have to convert them into paper or pixels. (From this point on, this will be known as The Paper or Pixel Principle.) Writing the idea down creates the recipe, the blueprint, the formula, the instructions, and the map.

I have notebooks filled with dreams stacked up in my house. I am certain that these notebooks are the most valuable items I own. They contain the descriptions, plans, and sketches of thousands of great ideas just waiting for Step 3!

Before we move on, it is essential to note that the more time you spend acting in Step 2, the easier the final step will be. In Step 2, you can start small with a few notes and descriptions. Then, come back early and often to flesh out your idea (please don't flush it out).

For example, if you're making a recipe, you write down the ingredients and where you need to shop for them. If you're building your dream home, sketch out a crude representation and a list of the specialists and the materials you'll need. Then list the resources that will fill in any gaps in your knowledge or abilities. If you need help financing your dream, this step is critical because it makes it real enough for others to see and support. It's exactly what makes Kickstarter work.

Step 3. Make it real.

Despite what you may think, this step is also easy when you follow the process. That is because you've already created your dream twice. First, you made it in your head when you identified your vision, and then you did it again when you wrote it down. Now you simply do the thing. You should have found the steps and functions required for progress in Step 2. If not, bounce back for a moment to write it out.

Keep moving. Dreams are like sharks. If either one stops moving, people make up sayings about them dying. So, as long as you work on one of the three steps, you're making progress. However, the goal must always be to move forward to the next step to complete the process.

LAST BITE

Whether your dream is to create a great BLT, a hilarious video, or a way to put a human on Mars, the steps are the same. Imagine it. Write it down. Make it real. There is no reason why you can't start today. And once you do, keep moving. You'll create something great. And when you do, send me a note to tell me all about it.

CHAPTER 54

Let Envy Be Your Guide.

MOST PEOPLE WILL tell you that envy is bad. They will say you should be happy with what you have. But don't believe them. Envy can be one of the most powerfully positive forces on Earth. It reveals what we truly enjoy, what we want most, and the people we want to be like. So don't feel bad about envy. Baby, you were born this way.

That said, it's best to use envy for good, and that starts with recognizing it as a powerful, and natural human instinct. Don't try to quiet that voice. Instead, tune in and try to learn what it can teach you. Envy is like a gravitational force pulling you towards your happiness.

"Envy (noun): a feeling of discontented or resentful longing aroused by someone else's possessions, qualities, or luck."

"Envy (verb): desire to have a quality, possession, or other desirable attribute belonging to someone else."

Envy is like an extra sense. It offers insight into feelings that are hard to articulate. To use envy for good, ask yourself questions like these:

- ▶ Do you envy the person who doesn't have to travel for work or the person who gets to travel for work?
- ▶ Do you envy your friend who has dinner with their family every night or the person who eats out more nights than not?
- ▶ Do you envy the entrepreneur? Or the volunteer? Or the activist?
- ▶ Do you envy the rich and famous?
- ▶ Do you envy the simple and anonymous life?

Your envy is trying to lead you on your true path. So don't protest too much. I've found myself attracted to and envious of all kinds of random things throughout my life. Instead of feeling bad about them or trying to turn the feelings off, I have tuned in and recognized the things I most want to have, do or be. The things I once envied have contributed greatly to my happiness.

Here is a quick list of random things I have envied:

- A pair of well-worn work boots
- High school classmates who could lift a lot of weights
- Entrepreneurs
- People who have canoes
- Families who take adventurous vacations
- Mountain climbers
- People who don't follow popular opinion
- People who have great blogs
- Volunteers

These things that I once envied, have now added a lot to my happiness. Instead of considering my feelings to be negative, I allowed them to motivate me. And I am grateful for them.

Today, my work boots are my favorite shoes to wear. I began lifting weights my freshman year in high school, and it has been the absolute best thing for my mental and physical health. I launched my agency in 2016, and I am eager to get to work each day. I own a beautiful 17 foot fiberglass canoe and three kayaks, all of which bring my family and me great joy. I have had several adventurous vacations with my wife and kids that have changed how we view the world. I've climbed many mountains and felt the rewards of accomplishment and enjoyed the views. I am confident in my unpopular ways.

I'm working on the blog thing. And I still have a nagging feeling that I don't volunteer enough and envy those who do.

LAST BITE

Don't regret your feelings of envy. Don't think you fail to measure up because you haven't accomplished the things you see others doing that you also want to achieve. Instead, add the things you envy and truly want to your list. Then create a plan to make them yours and get to work. (That's what I do. And someday, I expect to have/do/be all of them.)

CHAPTER 55

MY CAREER GOAL is to create the perfect advertising agency. Simple, right? Maybe not. Attaining perfection is hard. And elusive. But that's my goal because it is hard. And because achieving it would help make everyone involved, including my clients, my teammates, and our families happy, sought after, and prosperous.

If you are tackling something hard (and I hope you are), it will test you. Repeatedly. Like a diabetic tests their glucose. Your mission is like a boxing match. You step between the ropes and square off with whatever or whoever is standing between you and your goals. And you start throwing all you have at each other, knowing only one of you will win—the one who wants it more.

As you fight for your dreams, your goals, and your right to party, here's a quote that'll help. Pull it out between rounds and use it as your metaphorical packet of smelling salt to help shake off the cobwebs and the fatigue.

"Always bear in mind that your own resolution to success is more important than any other thing."
—Abraham Lincoln, from a letter written to Ishraim Reavis

My friend Abe Lincoln knew what he was talking about. Though he faced immense opposition, his resolution led to the single most important victory in American history, both for our nation and humanity. His unwavering resolve led to other lofty achievements. He's got his face on the penny, his name on a popular log-based toy, and he may or may not have collaborated on a car company with Matthew McConaughey.

Keep doing that hard thing. Keep fighting for your ultimate success. Keep your eyes on the prize. And keep Lincoln's quote close at hand. Because as he would attest, you never know when you might take an unexpected hit. (What? Too soon?)

LAST BITE

As Abraham Lincoln said (and showed), "...your own resolution to success is more important than any other thing."

CHAPTER 56

I USED TO think I was an honest person. I can only think of one promise that I've made and not kept since eighth grade. On the night I graduated from high school, I promised to sign my friend Simon Phillips' yearbook. And I still haven't done it. A few years ago, I reached out to Simon to apologize and complete my obligation. He had forgotten all about my unkept promise. I had not.

Smack dab in the middle of what I had considered a very honest life, I realized two shocking truths:

1. I tell lies all the time.
2. I have no idea how smack and dab came to represent the middle of something.

The lies I'm talking about are not little white lies. They are not exaggerations of something mostly true. I am talking about complete and utter falsifications and fabrications. Big league lies.

My string of outlandish lies goes back to high school. I remember claiming to be the boys' high school state record holder in the discus. At the time, I was a scrawny freshman who had only thrown the discus in one track meet. And in that one meet, my best throw was sixty feet shy of the state record! Yes, I was a liar. And my pants were certainly on fire.

The lies continued in college. After a couple of rough semesters academically, my GPA indicated that I was a terrible college student. But I lied and said that I was a great college student who got excellent grades and made the Dean's List. All lies.

Once I started my career in advertising, the lies just kept coming. Before I even landed a job, I started telling outlandish lies about my accomplishments, accolades, and income. I was a one-man lie-athon.

But a funny thing happened after I told those lies. They started coming true.

In the final track meet of my senior year, I broke the state high school discus record by three feet. In college, I followed up a couple of terrible academic semesters with seven straight semesters of earning a spot on the Dean's List, being named an Academic All-Big Ten athlete, and achieving at least a 3.5 GPA. In fact, I graduated with a 3.88 GPA for the coursework in my psychology and journalism double major.

In my advertising career, the lies have kept coming true, too. When I was a young writer, I lied when I said I could attract fun clients to the agency. But I did. Eventually, I helped the agency pick up Ski-Doo snowmobiles, SeaDoo watercraft, Evinrude outboard motors, as well as CanAm ATVs and the Spyder Roadster. Building on that success, I joined a relatively unknown regional agency and lied about how we would work with some of the world's best brands. And over the next few years, we won business with Nike, Coca-Cola, UPS, Nationwide, Chick-fil-A, and Wells Fargo.

The truth is, sometimes you need to lie in order to achieve great things. You have to believe the unbelievable to achieve the unachievable. That's some Jesse Jackson-worthy rhyming right there.

Even if you'd prefer to call it living into your dreams, positive thinking, envisioning, or autosuggestion, lying can be a powerful mental tool. If you can tell yourself something convincingly enough, you can make the lie a reality. And that is what I am doing on my quest to create the perfect agency. I will tell you that I'm the right person to do it. And that is a huge and completely unsubstantiated claim. AKA, a lie. Until it isn't.

I don't know of many other ways to make great things happen than to tell myself they will, even when there is no basis for it in reality. So I encourage you to try lying to yourself today.

LAST BITE

If you don't feel great, say you do. If you haven't achieved great things, say you have. Say it often. Every morning and every night, in the mirror. Lie to yourself. Lie until you don't even realize what the truth is anymore. And then make it all come true.

CHAPTER 57

I DON'T THINK that Scott Hauser, my former pastor, thinks much about advertising, branding, or marketing. But I do. So he may be surprised to hear how I interpreted one of his sermons.

One Sunday morning, Scott told a heartwarming story about two of his friends from Northwest Pennsylvania. His friends drove ten hours to Western (don't call me West) Virginia for a two hour memorial service for his mother-in-law. Directly after the service, the friends turned right around and drove ten hours home so they could make it to work the next day. What they did was so far beyond the expected that it was unreasonable.

Scott summarized the story with this simple statement: "Do something unreasonable. And people will never forget it."

In business, brand memorability is everything. If you are not top-of-mind when someone is considering a purchase or offering a recommendation, you have lost an opportunity. The best way to make sure you are top-of-mind is to do something that people will never forget. (And it's a real plus if that thing is also positive and legal.)

Too often in life, we focus on the fundamentals of blocking and tackling. It's certainly a rational and reasonable approach. But it can make us forget that one well-placed, well-intended, "nugget of crazy" may have more power than any carefully considered effort.

Your surprise doesn't have to be Red Bull level to make an impact. For example, I once ordered a t-shirt from Ames Bros, and when the package arrived, it came with a free sweatshirt! Not the other way around, which would have been reasonable. And now look at me, writing about Ames Bros because I'll never forget that surprise hoodie goodie.

Did you ever hear about the Ruth's Chris Steak House in Ann Arbor that offered a discount equivalent to the point difference in the final score of the 2016 Michigan-Rutgers college football game? Of course, they didn't expect Michigan to win by 78 points. But they honored it, and now they have a great, unreasonable story that sets them apart from other upscale steakhouse brands.

But here's the kicker. You have to act *before* you need the results. So do something today if you can.

Stunts, promotions, and customer service can all be highly memorable, as can charitable donations. My friend and fellow *Fletch* enthusiast, Jeff Hilimire, launched a great event called 48in48, which helps build 48 websites for nonprofit organizations in 48 hours, for free! That is completely unreasonable. And it's totally memorable.

If you haven't yet considered anything unreasonable, start now. This type of activity should be the most fun part of your day.

LAST BITE

The expected is invisible. The daring, the difficult, and the surprising stand out. If you want to be remembered, get noticed for moving beyond the norm to the wow.

CHAPTER 58

THERE IS NOTHING more valuable than a great idea. Powerful ideas can make you rich. They can make you famous. They can separate you from your competitors. Heck, they can convince people to buy a Pet Rock. The problem is, our lives are so freakin' busy. It can feel impossible to dedicate enough time for the focused thinking that will land you on *TechCrunch*, *Forbes*, or the Home Shopping Network.

When thinking time becomes scarce, I use a nighttime ideation technique that is so simple that it is almost laughable. I can confidently say that you're going to enjoy it more than diet and exercise combined. Are you ready?

GO TO BED 30 MINUTES EARLY.

Most of us push our bedtime to the very last minute. We either have tasks we want to accomplish before we throw in the towel at night or we work so hard the rest of the day that we finally want a little time to binge watch all the shows everyone else is talking about. Before you know it, the latest surprise on *The Story of Us, Stranger Things,* or *The Real Housewives of Roanoke* has robbed us of sleep. (Thanks a lot Andy Cohen.)

When I need more thinking time, I go to bed early. It sounds counterintuitive, but an amazing thing happens when you get your go-to-bed timing right. You will find that you are not so tired that you fall asleep immediately. You'll also find that it isn't so late that you stress about falling asleep before the alarm pounces on your head early the next morning. Instead, you can relax and enjoy the peace, calm, and comfort of your bed. And in that state, once you get good and quiet, the ideas come out to play.

To guide your creative thinking in that relaxed, pre-sleep state, imagine you're gently grabbing the topic you want to think about and softly placing it at the center of your mind. Then follow the inklings. They are the faint pathways that connect your central topic to new ideas, plans, and partnerships.

Remarkable solutions and innovations are born in that quiet time if we listen. To avoid interruption, you must leave your phone and other digital distractions in another room. An ill-timed push notification from Groupon about a sweet deal on "Naked Skydiving and Go-Karting for Four!" will interrupt your flow and kill an idea in the embryonic state. Instead, keep a notebook and pen on your nightstand to capture your ideas before they escape into the darkness.

If you'd like proof of concept, here's a real-world, bed-born idea that made a major financial impact. Ski-Doo snowmobiles was one of my favorite clients of all time. Unfortunately, a problem that had plagued much of the snowmobile industry for many years was creating a challenge for them as well. The mechanism that enabled a snowmobile to go in reverse added cost and weight to the sled. One night, while lying in bed, one of the Ski-Doo engineers wondered if he simply reversed the wiring on the engine, if the engine and subsequently the whole sled, would run in reverse. When he rushed in to work the next day to see if his idea would work, he was delighted to find that it did exactly what he had envisioned. And thus, the Rotax Electronic Reverse (RER) was born. Suddenly Ski-Doo could offer reversing capability on all of their snowmobiles without adding any additional weight or expense to the machine. The feature was a clear differentiator and competitive advantage that came from the bedroom, not the boardroom.

LAST BITE

The challenges of life and work can seem relentless. They come at us like chocolates barrelling down the conveyor belt towards Lucy and Ethel. But game changing ideas are out there waiting. To catch them, just lie down, be quiet, and let them come to you.

CHAPTER 59

If You Can Learn To Double Dutch, You Can Learn Anything.

STARTING SOMETHING NEW is hard. (I'm not just talking about going to prison for the first time. Which I imagine is really hard at first. And in the middle. And towards the end.) It's hard to be a rookie at anything. Some people enjoy the luxury of not caring whether or not they look dumb doing something new. I don't have that luxury. I care.

But I also really enjoy taking on new challenges. And I have developed a technique for starting new activities that you may find useful. I refer to it as my Double Dutch technique.

You remember Double Dutch. It's the playground activity where you try to jump two ropes, swinging simultaneously, in opposite directions. (Because jumping one swinging rope just isn't hard enough.) Double Dutch can be an intimidating activity.

Those ropes relentlessly nip at your heels. And once they bite your foot, the game immediately halts and brings everyone's attention to your failure.

But I like Double Dutch. It's an activity for people who like to try hard things. It's much more challenging than single Dutch or non-Dutch rope jumping. And it's infinitely tougher than just jumping up and down with no rope. (Which always earns you funny looks.)

Trying hard things is great for you. It makes you feel stronger, more confident, and more capable. It makes you feel like you are growing. And growth-minded people like to spend time with others who enjoy pushing themselves, too.

I use the Double Dutch technique all the time as I grow my advertising agency. Not only am I taking on new challenges personally, but I also want our team to continuously expand our capabilities and find new and better ways to help our clients.

Here's How the Double Dutch Technique Works:

1. Get close to the activity.

To get a feel for Double Dutch, you have to step into that space right next to the ropes. When I start something new, I try to get really close to the action first, without fully engaging. There is something about close proximity that helps you absorb how it works more quickly. If you want to climb Mt. Everest, go to basecamp first to get acclimated.

2. Watch others.

Aside from the very first Double Dutchers on earth, who I assume were twins from Amsterdam, no one has ever tried jumping the two-ropes-of-doom without first watching someone else do it. That's why I always watch other people performing the task I want to learn. I study the jumpers' moves, their attitudes, and their techniques. It's much like the way an actor studies others when preparing to play a role.

3. Find the rhythm.

Double Dutch has a unique rhythm all its own. You have to get in sync with it to succeed. Most human interactions are like this. For example, the interactions in networking events, yoga classes, and business meetings all follow a particular flow and cadence. Pay attention to them so you can anticipate the order and timing of the activities.

4. Jump in.

At some point, if you want to Double Dutch, you have to jump in. Once I have armed myself reasonably well by getting close to an activity, watching it, and finding the rhythm, I channel my inner David Lee Roth and jump (might as well). Sometimes it goes well from the start. Other times I need a mulligan.

5. Recalibrate.

In Double Dutch, the rope tells you what you did wrong. And the problem is always that you touched the rope. The question is where. Use that feedback to do better on the next try. If you jumped too soon, wait for another beat. If you jumped too late, go a bit sooner. This is little data at its best. Create a new plan based on the learnings.

6. Jump in again. And again.

To jump ropes, you have to keep trying. This is how life works. Get in and jump over and over until you get it right. Whether you want to build a great brand, learn how to knit, or run QuickBooks, there is ultimately no substitute for doing. Be a do-er.

LAST BITE

As you focus on growth and acquiring new skills, use the Double Dutch technique. Give yourself a chance to get close, observe, absorb, try, learn, and try again. Soon you will find yourself in rhythm, jumping, and singing, "Big Mac, Filet-O-Fish, Quarter Pounder, French Fries."

CHAPTER 60

ON A SUNDAY afternoon, my wife and I went on a rare date to the grocery store. It must have been a thing that day because we ran into our friends Tricia and Dan, who were also on a grocery date. The four of us talked for a few minutes until we were interrupted by some grocery store drama.

Another couple, apparently on their own grocery store date, was walking down the aisle when one of them knocked a large bottle of cooking oil off of the shelf and onto the floor. True to its name, the shatterproof bottle did not shatter. But when the bottle hit the floor, the flip-cap lid flipped open.

And suddenly, cooking oil, in all of its golden glory, glugged onto the floor in the grocery store's busiest intersection. It was like the grocery store equivalent of the Deepwater Horizon well spewing oil into the Gulf of Mexico.

A crowd of Sunday shoppers stopped to watch the drama unfold.

As the oil continued to pulse out of the bottle, the corn oil slick grew larger and larger. You could practically hear Florence Henderson's heart breaking over this loss of perfectly good Wesson.

The couple that caused the oil-cident stood motionless over the oozing mess. Then the man said, "We need to tell them there has been a spill." Then, as the corn oil continued to flow like midwestern lava across the grocery store floor, he repeated with more concern and more volume, "We need to tell them there has been a spill!"

After the man shouted, I realized he was not in a state of mind to end this crisis. Visions of the Exxon Valdez disaster filled my head. I imagined helpless birds covered in oil. And I thought, "not on my watch!"

I was standing twenty feet away from the epicenter of the oil spill when I sprang into action. Where others may have fled from the disaster, thinking only of their safety and cleanliness, I walked toward the expanding oil spill. I was running on a cocktail of instinct and adrenaline. When I reached ground zero, I reached down, grabbed the bottle, and set it upright.

Suddenly, the oil stopped spilling. The disaster was contained. And shoppers resumed shopping. It was the simplest and most effective thing anyone could have done to mitigate the issue. A toddler could have recognized the solution and had both the mental and physical capacity to upright that fallen bottle to stop the flow of corn oil.

Yet, the adult male at the center of the crisis could only think that someone needed to hear that there was a problem. And his female companion stared, motionless, unable to process her next move.

When you see a problem or create a problem, don't just pass it along to someone else. Act to solve it. Work to reduce it. Do what you can to prevent it from getting worse. To watch a preventable problem spread without lifting a finger to stop it is irresponsible. Don't just announce that there is a fire. Throw some water on it.

Take responsibility for the problems you face. Imagine you are the only one who can address them. Then do it. Develop a bias towards decision-making and action. Those biases help you get things done. They help you solve problems. And they make you a more valuable employee, friend, and neighbor.

LAST BITE

When things go wrong, don't just report the problem. Instead, be part of the solution. Diagnose quickly. Think quickly. Act quickly. Focus on what you can do. Then do it without delay. It will help prevent a small mishap from becoming a massive problem.

CHAPTER 61

Always Play The Host.

WE'VE ALL BEEN told not to talk to strangers. But I love strangers. (The stranger, the better.) Maybe it's because I moved a lot as a kid. It meant I regularly found myself amongst people I didn't know. I understood that if I didn't talk to strangers, I would have no one to talk to.

Most people are less comfortable with total strangers than I am. That's probably a good human survival mechanism, but it's a mechanism I lack. As a business founder, I know that being able to talk to strangers is critical for entrepreneurs. If you don't talk to strangers, you are not growing your business or helping anyone else grow theirs. When I meet a potential new client, our ability to connect as humans is what leads to us working together.

In her book *How to Work a Room: The Ultimate Guide to Making Lasting Connections—In Person and Online,* Susan RoAne shares great insights on approaching a room full of strangers. One of her most interesting and important ideas to know is this:

When people find themselves with other people they don't know, they adopt one of two behaviors:

1. A guest mindset.
2. A host mindset.

The guest mindset adopts the attitude of the person who waits for others to make the first move. They wait to be introduced, welcomed, or fed. They pause to join or participate until they receive an invitation. If you have a party full of people with guest mindsets, you don't have a party.

The host mindset initiates. They welcome others, introduce them to other guests, offer them food or drink, or take a crack at catching the greased pig (depending on your event). You activate the party. If you want to feel at home and enjoy any group of strangers, adopt a host mindset.

This is what I do. I just didn't have a name for it before I read Susan RoAne's book. I don't wait for someone else to decide whether or not I am worthy of conversation. I don't want to give anyone else that power over me. So I make the first move. I create the introduction. I act as if it were my job to make people feel welcome.

I've found that when you don't worry about rejection, you don't get rejected. Think of it as a junior high dance. You just have to walk up to someone and say, 'Stairway to Heaven' is a sweet tune. Let's dance. And let's not worry about the fact that this song will gradually speed up, and we're going to go from a slow dance into a full-on rock song, and we won't know when we should stop holding on to each other." Remember the Stairway analogy because holding on to one person too long at a social gathering also becomes awkward.

If you want to enjoy a room full of strangers more, ditch your stranger danger senses. Adopt a host mindset. Act like it's your party, wedding, conference, or luncheon. Start by introducing yourself to others. Ask people about themselves. Here are a few starters:

- So, where are you from?
- What do you do for work?
- Where did you go to school?
- How do you know {party giver's name}?
- Why are your palms so sweaty?
- Why the neck tattoo?

There are people at every gathering who are just dying for someone else to make the first move. They haven't realized that they should be making the first move. Maybe it's because they never read this book or *How to Work a Room*, or because they never danced with me in junior high. Help them out. Be a host. You might discover they are extremely interesting or valuable. If they're not comfortable initiating, you'll have to be. You'll enjoy the rewards. Because you never know when that total stranger may have the kindness, connection, or kidney you need.

LAST BITE

The host becomes the leader. They make good and memorable things happen. They make uncomfortable situations comfortable. Everyone can play host, but few do. If you do, you will have the ability to create the world you want to live in.

CHAPTER 62

Do Small Things With Big Bangs.

THE WORLD IS full of lazy people. You can find them in schools, government jobs, businesses, and superglued to couches. They are in every sector of society. And they are easy to spot because they don't move very fast.

At the opposite end of the human spectrum from the lazy people, you will find the "Rise and Grind" crowd, the "Everyday I'm Hustling" crowd, and the "I'll Sleep When I'm Dead" crowd. Many of us self-identify with these more aggressive, work-hard-play-hard types. But there is a surprising reality you should know.

Sometimes lazy people outperform the hard-chargers.

Wait. What? How could it be possible that the tree sloths sometimes outperform the workhorses? How does a sleepy koala beat a busy beaver? The lazy but successful crowd has a secret that you need to know.

The Lazy Person's Key To Success:
Do small things that create big bangs.

It is easy to keep busy without getting ahead. Have you ever watched a human doggy paddle in the water? It's not pretty. By swimming doggy-style, humans create a lot of motion but make very little progress. Don't do this. It is a waste of time and energy.

Instead, do the little things that create an enormous impact. Remember the Pareto Principle, also known as the 80/20 rule or the Law of the Vital Few. Whatever you call it, it means that 80% of effects (outputs) come from 20% of causes (inputs). And that means that you can be lazy *and* successful if you focus on the small tasks that generate large results.

Examples of Small Tasks With Big Returns:

1. Make the right phone calls
2. Ask the right questions
3. Ask for what you want
4. Show up
5. Know a guy
6. Read the directions
7. Pay attention
8. Connect dots
9. Be seen
10. Create a top 10 list and put it in a book for successful people

You don't have to work hard to be successful. The quality of your actions far outweighs the quantity. By doing small things that provide a big bang, you use minimum force to create maximum results. Find the small activities in your world that make the greatest impact. Then perform them repeatedly. It's not lazy, it's efficient and effective.

But always remember, when the *Rise-and-Grinders* also do the small things with large consequences, they eat lazy people for breakfast. Pass the syrup.

LAST BITE

Not all actions are the same. Find the ones that make the biggest impact, and do those first. Or make only those actions. You will be amazed at how much you can accomplish.

CHAPTER 63

I WANT YOU to try an experiment. Over the next 24 hours, note how many people you encounter that you don't know. I warn you, it may freak you out. Most of us live anonymously in a sea of strangers. They are everywhere. (Like minivans.) And we have become immune to these strangers who surround us. It's almost as if they disappear when we ignore them. (Like reality TV stars.)

At my gym recently, I got a reminder of my anonymity. After I scanned my membership card, the guy who routinely works at the reception desk said, "have a good day, man."

Most normal people would smile and do just that. Not me. Instead, I had a flashback to college. I was a freshman at the University of Wisconsin and a member of the track team. As I was at the McClain Center lifting weights, one of the football players whom I saw daily walked through the room. When he passed by, he said, "Hey! What's up, man?" I replied with something like, "Hey, Man. What's up?" I thought nothing of it.

But then he stopped and asked, "What is your name?"

I said, "Adam." (My go-to answer.)

We shook hands. He said, "My name's Aaron. Enough of this bullshit, saying, 'Hey man.' or 'What's up, bro?' F-that! I see you here every day. We should know each other's names!"

Aaron 'Scrappy' Norvell was right. It was bullshit that we would repeatedly see each other, even greet each other, and not know each other's names. And after this introduction, he was no longer just a guy I saw. He was a guy I knew named Aaron. The difference was, and is, profound.

I suspect I wasn't the only person Scrappy made an effort to get to know by name (he currently has 4,981 friends on Facebook). He is funny, outgoing, and entertaining. We would see a lot of each other over the next few years in Madison. Today, he is an actor in Hollywood. If you ever need to cast a police officer, Obama look-alike, former college linebacker, or someone who can deliver the line, "Hey, what's your name?", Scrappy is your guy.

Now, back to the story.

With this random flashback playing in my head, I asked the guy working at the counter at Elite Sports Club, "what's your name?"

He replied, "Andrew."

I responded, "My name is Adam." (Still my go-to.)

We shook hands. Now, every time I walk into the gym, we greet each other by name. We have real conversations instead of awkward "Hey-man" nods.

Every person we encounter in business, at social gatherings, and at the grocery store is either an Insider or an Outsider. The difference is whether or not we know each other by name. That sense of familiarity and friendship that can only develop once you know a person's name makes an enormous difference on this planet. Especially because we are so often surrounded by John and Jane Does. (Does is supposed to be Doe-plural. But it looks like Does, doesn't it?)

Working in advertising, we often encounter people we don't have to know by name. The receptionists who greet us when we visit a client. The people who sit next to the conference rooms where we gather and make noise. The IT person who inevitably saves the presentation. I want to meet them, so I make a habit of introducing myself. Suddenly, we are not just people who see each other regularly, but people who know each other by name.

LAST BITE

Convert more of those people you see or say hello to regularly, into people you actually know by name. It's easy. Introduce yourself and ask for their name in return. Write their names down. Start a list with a description of who they are on your phone or in a notebook. Refer back to the list when necessary. The rewards are profound.

CHAPTER 64

Initiate, Connect, And Reconnect.

I RECENTLY WATCHED the movie *Green Book*. The film is about the unlikely friendship between an African-American classical pianist and the blue-collar caucasian man hired to drive him on tour through the 1960s American South. The movie is enjoyable, and I recommend it. The highlight is a line delivered by Viggo Mortensen's character. It jumped off the screen and sucker punched me in the earhole.

> *"The world is full of lonely people afraid to make the first move."*
> — Frank "Tony Lip" Vallelonga, *Green Book*

On a planet of almost seven and a half billion people, none of us should feel lonely. Yet we often do. Most people wish they had more, deeper, better, or more fulfilling personal and professional connections. But we fail to recognize that the easiest way to make this happen is to make the first move.

If you want more or better professional contacts, be the one who makes contact. You are the one who should make the first phone call, send the first text, or write the first email. It's that simple.

If you want to connect, you should do the connecting. It doesn't matter if you are reconnecting with your high school friends, your cousins, or your former co-workers from that place where everyone bonded over the stupid boss. The average smartphone offers at least a dozen ways to make this happen. If you are not weird (there is no guarantee that you are not), chances are good that others will be happy to reconnect with you, too.

8 Easy Ways to Create New Connections or Reconnect Old Ones:

1. Coffee/Chocolate Milk Meetings

You don't have to drink coffee. I don't. Heck, you can eat caramels or enjoy them apples. It's all arbitrary. #namethatfilm

2. After-work Happy Hours

My friend, Susan Stearns, has a super-strong happy hour game. She gets a group of former co-workers together a few times a year. Thanks for making the first move, SS.

3. Book Clubs

Two of my friends, Betty Garrot and Stacy Sollenberger, are bookworms. Both of them are in three book clubs right now. These gatherings are not only great ways to facilitate social interactions, but they also improve your bookmarking skills.

4. Dinner Parties

These are a great way to jumpstart or turbocharge personal relationships. My neighbors Yassir and Ghada are excellent at this.

5. Video Conference Meetups

I created a monthly video meetup with my college track teammates. It's now a highlight of my month. "On Wisconsin!"

6. Group Texts

Several of my high school classmates and I have a group text that regularly flares up with jokes. Like it did this week when our classmate Dan Richards was interviewed on NPR. Thanks to Marcus Chioffi for starting that one!

7. Restaurant or Bar Meetings

In the course of two days in Atlanta, I met with ten different people at restaurants; Stephanie Herbst-Lucke, Diana Keough, Theresa and Jabari Pride, Harper Cornell, Nicola Smith, Scott Jenkins, Heather Hudgins, Kim Hoey, and Mark O'Brien. I am pretty good at this game. (And lucky that people agree to meet me.)

8. Hike or Bike with Others

The healthy way to multitask. It's kind of the opposite of option seven.

Never in history have people lived so close together, had such phenomenal resources to facilitate interactions, and yet felt so isolated. It's bullshiznit. And it's all because most people are longing for someone else to make the first move.

Don't wait. Initiate. We're in a golden age for human connection. Try this. Create an alumni group that consists of people from a school, employer, program, or organization you enjoyed. Invite people to be part of the group and watch how positively they respond.

Form a group around shared interests. Develop a professional organization of people who do what you do. Be the spark. Be the glue. Heck, be the whole dang craft closet that brings the project to life. And see what happens next.

I have long considered Fridays to be "Phone-A-Friend Fridays". It means that every Friday, I contact someone I haven't talked to in a long time. You can do this, too. You are sure to surprise and delight someone. All while reducing global loneliness levels.

LAST BITE

There is nothing more important to your personal and professional happiness than meaningful connections with other humans. Don't hesitate to make the first call, text, or send the first smoke signal. Start today because we all get ahead when we get together.

CHAPTER 65

Lean On Others To Accomplish More.

I COME FROM a large family. Actually, I come from two large families. My mom is one of nine children. My dad is one of 12. Both sides of my family have made family a priority. Not only have they committed to a lot of procreating, they have also committed to a lot of recreating, too.

Both the Albrechts and the Spraus have made pilgrimages to the Snow Mountain Ranch in Winter Park, Colorado. It's rated the #1 location in America for family reunions. (Although how one mountain in Colorado is known as Snow Mountain confounds me. Don't all of Colorado's mountains have snow?)

Family bonding and team building are the focus (the foci?) of our reunions. We stay in large family cabins that house 40 to

80 people each. We play together, eat together, and enjoy general togetherness together.

On one of the days at each reunion, we participate in organized teambuilding exercises. The ranch offers activities that require you to learn how to work with a partner or an entire team to complete a challenge.

One of my favorite challenges is the partner cable walk. In this challenge, two partners stand on separate cables suspended eighteen inches off the ground. Facing each other, the partners have to move as far along the cable as possible without falling off. The kicker is that the cables are arranged in a V-shape, so they spread farther and farther apart as you walk.

When we took on this challenge several years ago with my Mom's family, I sat back and observed the other pairs as they navigated the cables. Remember the Double Dutch technique? I studied what worked and what didn't.

The best performance (farthest distance traveled) came from my brother-in-law Uriah, and my cousin Jacci's husband, Mike. If you laid Uriah and Mike end to end (which, to my knowledge, we have never done) they would be close to thirteen feet long. All things being equal, height was a major advantage.

But all things are not equal. I quickly spotted what I thought people were doing wrong. All of the pairs began by holding hands and then inching down the cables. While holding on to each other seemed like a good strategy, eventually, it became limiting.

Using the insights from our observations, my wife Dawn and I took our turn. Unlike everyone else, we didn't hold on to each other. Instead, we leaned against each other. As we started, we looked as if we were doing standing push-ups against each other. Or maybe we looked like we got caught playing Patty Cake with crazy glue on our palms.

As we made our way along the V-shaped cables, we became a human hinge, with our hands forming the connection point. As the cables formed a large and expanding V-shape, Dawn and I also formed a V-shape that matched the angle of the cables. This shape made all the difference. Our lean-on-me technique enabled us to travel twice as far as any other pair. Or pear. Or Pierre.

It is easy to think we are teaming up with others when we are side-by-side in the same environment, but proximity and contact are not enough. You have to reorient yourself to rely on your partners or teammates to do their jobs. You have to sacrifice your posture to create a stronger team, machine, company, or partnership.

As we grow The Weaponry, we need to continue building and operating as an interdependent team. To thrive, we need to create a scalable organization that gets larger, and broader, and deeper to accommodate the increase in demand. And that means that each of our members must do what is best for the entire team. And each of us must be able to trust our teammates to do their jobs without hand-holding. It is the only way to achieve our ambitious goals.

It is certainly true within our marriages. Since our first date, my wife Dawn and I have been leaning on each other and accomplishing more together than we ever could have on our own. Just like we did on the partner cable walk at the family reunion in Colorado.

LAST BITE

For the whole to be greater than the sum of its parts, we can't simply hold on to each other. Instead, we must lean on each other, trusting that our teammates will lean back on us. By creating this dynamic, we produce a support structure that gets the best results. It's true at work, in athletics, and in families.

CHAPTER 66

Focus On Your Most Important Thing And Make It King.

DO YOU KNOW why you are successful? I know why I am. Since you are reading this book, I suspect you want to learn to be more successful, too. So let's get right to it.

After this distraction. And another distraction. Wow, so many distractions! These distractions are ruining this paragraph! Or maybe they are demonstrating the point of this chapter.

The common theme of my greatest successes, and the greatest successes of many others in history, comes down to one word — "focus".

Throughout my career, I have created the best work, come up with the best answers, and had the most impact on my clients when I focused on the challenge. The same holds true for personal successes and achievements.

Far too often, we take on too many responsibilities concurrently. We juggle and reorder them like Lucy and Ethel in the chocolate factory. Frantically and unproductively. Taking on too much at once dilutes your power, potential, and performance. Focus concentrates your energy.

FOCUS = Focus On Completely Until Solved

Focus means prioritizing. It means scheduling so that the essential things can be the star for a time. Sometimes that means we focus on projects exclusively for a month. Sometimes it means focusing on a challenge for a couple of days. Or a couple of hours.

Multitasking is a myth so popular that it won the Myth America Pageant. Avoid it at all costs. Multitasking creates the illusion of productivity. But the work is shallow and the rapid task switching prevents you from ever achieving remarkable results.

Scheduling to eliminate distractions is necessary. Maximize focus. More focus means greater intensity of thought, deeper evaluation, and more intelligent solutions.

I have won major pieces of new business and have created work that helped transform the way a brand behaved and spurred transformational growth. In every case, those victories have come after I cleared my plate, my desk, and my brainium to get the work done. So as we attack clients' challenges, I am always thinking about focus. I want to deploy the thinking power of each member of our team in a way that drives the most remarkable client results. It's why we schedule work to give every project center stage for the appropriate amount of time.

Distractions aren't just a work thing. They're everywhere. Volunteering, attending events, and getting roped into activities in your personal life can detract from your focus, too.

It can be tempting to take on as much as one human can shoulder to show how tough, capable, or responsible you are. You might appear helpful to your team and your employer, but in reality, this load-it-until-the-axles-bend approach doesn't lead to a superstar performance that makes you proud. (It will, however, lead to broken axles.)

LAST BITE

Micro-focus moves the needle micrometers. Macro-focus can move it miles. So if you are looking for better performance, ideas, and results, find a way to better focus on the project in front of you.

CHAPTER 67

Block Your Calendar To Put Time To Work For You.

WHEN I WAS a student-athlete, my schedule was booked solid. I was in class every day by 8:55 am. Classes lasted until 2 pm. At 2:30 pm, I was at track practice. I left practice at 6 pm and went to dinner. I ate at the Sports Buffet until they kicked me out at 7 pm. By 7:20 pm I was in the library studying in the quiet section (seriously). By 10:30 pm, I was taking the 'Drunk Bus' home.

Something magical was working for me during this time. I had large chunks of time with completely focused effort. I started the day focused on my classes. Then track practice. Then on eating (which felt like a job because I was the smallest discus thrower in the Big Ten Conference, but trying hard not to be). And finally, on studying.

These four time blocks helped me focus my undivided attention on my biggest life goals. (It may have helped that there were no smartphones back then to distract me with an Instagram feed full of hilarious Pro Wrestling fails. @Wrestlebotch)

I still use the type of focused scheduling I employed as a student-athlete today. As a result, I hope to achieve the same level of productivity, growth, and progress that I enjoyed two decades ago. It's why I time block my calendar to create deep focus on my most important tasks, that will help me achieve my long-term goals.

The Time Blocks on my Calendar:

- ▶ An hour of blocked writing time every morning from 6:10 am - 7:10 am
- ▶ Two hours of totally focused work on my most important tasks from 10 am - 12 pm
- ▶ A regular one-hour lunch from 12 pm - 1 pm, which also helps keep my energy high and prepares me for more afternoon sessions of total focus
- ▶ One hour of total focus on my most important issues in the afternoon from 2 pm - 3 pm
- ▶ Dedicated open time for meetings, calls, and emails to start and end the day
- ▶ A 30-minute planning session every Sunday night to plan the most important tasks for the week, to help me achieve my long-term goals

It is not enough to have goals. You need to put in the work required to achieve them. That's why it is so important to devote large chunks of time on your calendar to focus on your most important tasks every day.

LAST BITE

Remember, scheduling your time costs nothing. But you'll enjoy the dividends from achieving your goals for generations.

CHAPTER 68

TODAY, MILLIONS OF people will be robbed by their co-workers. This thievery is the most under reported crime in America. The perpetrators are not stealing your cash, phones, or heirloom-quality Tupperware from the breakroom fridge. What they are stealing is far more valuable.

They are stealing your time.

Time is your most precious commodity and people take it from you every day. They stop by your desk to chat for too long. They cause meetings and phone calls to go longer than necessary. They turn their lack of planning into your emergency. Before you know it, the whistle blows, Fred Flintstone slides down his dinosaur, and it's time to go home. And you've spent eight hours of your life at work, but your most important work is not yet done.

McGruff the Time Dog is here to tell you that you have got to protect your time. If you want to make a valuable contribution to your organization, your family, or your community, you need precious time.

As a business owner, I look for spare time like spare change in my couch cushions. Because every time I find a few extra minutes, it enables me to spend time working on my most important tasks. I can use that valuable time to create new products or services, improve processes and find ways to deliver better work for our clients. But that all takes time.

It is easy to spend all of your time dealing with the needs of others. It may even feel like you are busy working. But you are not advancing your projects. You'll look back at the end of the year and see that you did little to promote your most important initiatives.

Protecting your time means finding and protecting hours of uninterrupted progress. That may mean working from home, a coffee shop, or Chick-fil-A (my secret work spot).

Consider blocking off large chunks of time on your calendar so that no one schedules you up. And it may mean putting a sign up in your office space that says you are working on something really important and can't be interrupted. Make a habit of turning off your email, Slack, and phone. In the digital age, people have more ways than ever to get sneaky and steal your time.

It's great to be a team player. But you can't let others take away your scoring opportunities. That's what happens when you sit in meetings too long, are regularly interrupted, or get sent on a wild goose chase. (Ever notice that no one ever chases the domesticated geese?)

Don't be afraid to be selfish with your time. It's the only way to advance the work that you are directly responsible for doing. It also keeps your work at work. And it prevents you from having to steal time from your personal life to get your work finished.

LAST BITE

Protect your time and then, crank away on your most important work, uninterrupted. If you can find time to do this every day, you'll be amazed at how much you can accomplish each week.

CHAPTER 69

IN SEVENTH GRADE, I had a social studies teacher named Mr. Wilson. I remember Mr. Wilson as a portly, middle-aged white man. But it wouldn't surprise me if I discovered that he was the same age I am now. When you are 12, you think all adults are old.

Like most teachers, Mr. Wilson had go-to phrases that we repurposed into hilarious impressions when he wasn't around. In fairness, we made hilarious impressions of all of our teachers. It's probably why I never wanted to be a teacher.

Several times in every class, while we were supposed to be working on our assignments, Mr. Wilson would bellow, "T.O.T!" He was not announcing his craving for tater tots (at least, I don't think so). "T.O.T" was an acronym for Time on Task. When my friend Marcus Chioffi (rhymes with coffee) and I would hear "T.O.T.", we would snicker at how much Mr. Wilson sounded like our impression of Mr. Wilson.

Today, I find myself thinking about T.O.T. a lot. As I reflect on what has worked for me throughout my career and entrepreneurial journey, I keep coming back to T.O.T.

We all have dreams, goals, and aspirations. But we tend to spend far too little time working on them to force them into reality. The amount of time you spend working on a task is the key determinant of success in that area. There simply is no substitute for focused work. It is why Time on Task is the key to progress.

LAST BITE

If you want to be an entrepreneur or achieve any lofty goal, you have to spend "Time on Task". Focus your time. Block it. Invest in it. Remove distractions. And then do the work. Keep your T.O.T. It's the only way to make great things happen. Just like Mr. Wilson said.

CHAPTER 70

Investments In Growth Pay Out The Most.

MY FIRST JOB in advertising paid me $21,000 a year. I wasn't sure how I was going to eat, but I was thrilled to be a professional copywriter. I was raking in that thin dough for three months before it surged to $22,000. I was making it drizzle. Six months later, I got another bump to $24,000. I bought a used Toyota 4-Runner with 175,000 miles on it. Eighteen months after I had started my first job, my salary climbed to $30,000. Ever since then, I have felt rich. Seriously.

None of those salary adjustments made me any more valuable to my employer. They spent money on me because I was good at my job. (And because they had underpaid for my value from the start.)

As I look back at my career, there was one investment that an employer made in me that truly made me a more valuable asset to them. In April of 2000, the advertising agency I worked for, Cramer Krasselt, sent me to a seminar in Chicago led by Toni Louw on presenting creative work. It cost $240 and it made the agency more money than the salary they paid me. By far.

At this one-day seminar, I learned how to see creative work from the client's perspective. I learned about persuasion, pre-selling, and demonstration. I learned about storytelling, building a case for the work we were proposing, and developing logical conclusions.

I learned about showmanship and being a good host to clients. I learned about how to turn a passive audience into an actively engaged audience. I was hooked.

After tearing a hole in my khakis on the train ride from Milwaukee to Chicago, I also learned that I could sew a rip in my pants, in a bathroom stall, in less than five minutes using a sewing kit I asked for at the hotel lobby.

The timing could not have been better. I had three years of experience, which was enough time to know a few things and enough experience to recognize what I had been doing wrong. And I still had the majority of my career to get it right.

I soaked up the ideas and techniques like a Shop-Vac. Presenting was already one of my favorite parts of the job. Now, I had a great base of theory and technique to build on.

When I got home, I typed up everything I had learned and added two scoops of personal style. Suddenly, I had a game plan and a process for evaluating client-worthy creative ideas. And I knew how to present them effectively and make them entertaining. (Although my entertainment may be more Branson than Broadway.)

Within two months, I had the perfect opportunity to put my new skills to use. The Ski-Doo snowmobile account went up for review. Because of my passion for snowmobiling and enthusiasm for the opportunity, I got to lead the creative charge for the pitch. I was only 26 years old.

I poured myself into the Ski-Doo pitch. Through a combination of drive, my seminar learnings, and great teammates, we put on quite a show. Not only did we win the account, but we also proceeded to pitch and win the other Bombardier Recreational Products (BRP) brands too. Those included Sea-Doo, Evinrude, and Johnson Outboards motors, CanAm ATVs, and the CanAm Spyder.

Pitching and business development became core strengths. And despite my early career concerns, I continued to eat regularly.

Today, I own an ad agency. As I consider investments in my fast-growing business, I reflect on the ROI of that $240 seminar fee. It advanced my skills and abilities. It helped me win new business and grow the agency substantially. It made the agency money. All the returns made me a much more valuable resource to the agency.

LAST BITE

It may be more fun to spend money on cappuccino machines, murals, and foosball tables, but if you want to enjoy a huge return on your money, invest in growing your people. This includes yourself. Make your strengths stronger and your breadths broader. Provide the tools that you and your people need to realize your full potential. Money spent on growth will yield a greater return than any other investment you will ever make.

CHAPTER 71

WOULDN'T IT BE nice if everything in life worked according to your schedule? You simply set the amount of time you need to handle personal or professional tasks and nothing would challenge your pre-established timeline. That would be pleasant. And it would bore me to tears.

The world doesn't conform to your schedule. Business, and life, are far too unpredictable. As Nationwide Insurance used to say, "life comes at you fast".

Opportunities and threats appear in a blink. In the social media era, you need to respond before today's opportunities become yesterday's tweets. You must be able to thwart threats before they become wildfires, engulfing your home, business, and (God forbid) your Wi-Fi.

But opportunities abound in imperfect schedules. As a business founder, I am always thrilled by quick deadlines. They add excitement to the work. They test our abilities. They push us to learn what we can do and what we can do without.

Ridiculous deadlines present favorable conditions for creativity, too. When time is short, the approval process is also short. You run through fewer approvers, and they tend to be more accepting of really great creative solutions. So better ideas are often produced under tight timelines because the client has less time for second-guessing.

But it isn't just small business owners (and mothers) who have to respond to last-minute requests and short deadlines. If you don't believe me, consider this story from Neal Gabler's book, *Walt Disney: The Triumph of the American Imagination.*

In 1963 the team at Disneyland received a crazy request from the Executives at Pepsi. Pepsi had been working on a collaboration with UNICEF for the upcoming 1964 World's Fair in New York, but had failed to come up with a worthwhile idea. So they approached the creative team at Disney with the daunting task of creating an exhibit to fill their 94,000 square foot exhibit space. Unfortunately, they had far too little time and far too little money for the challenge. So Joe Fowler, the supervisor at Disneyland, turned down their request.

When Walt Disney heard this news, he was furious. He said, "I'll make those decisions!" and informed his team that they would indeed take on the Pepsi project. To solve the time, space, and money challenges, Disney devised a boat ride through a canal, surrounded by animated dolls from around the world. The dolls sang a song that Disney commissioned the Sherman brothers to write. As Disney described the concept of the exhibit to the Shermans, he explained, "It's a small world after all." And that, of course, became the name of the song and the ride itself.

The World's Fair exhibit was a resounding success for Pepsi and UNICEF. Today, almost 55 years later, that boat ride is still one of the most popular attractions at Disney World. And its theme song is known around the world.

LAST BITE

Your next great opportunity may show up at your doorstep wearing a really short deadline. But don't be too quick to shoo it away. Don't focus on all the reasons you can't take on the challenge. Focus on the possibilities. That opportunity just may turn into the greatest thing you've ever done.

CHAPTER 72

WHAT WOULD YOU do if nothing scared you? Would you wrestle a rabid alligator? Be the first person on the dance floor? Invite a family of termites to your log cabin for a long weekend? Or would you do something even scarier, like change career paths in your prime?

If you were fearless, you would be unstoppable. But fear is the greatest tranquilizer on Earth. It can stop a talented human like you in your tracks. Fear can prevent you from becoming the amazing person you were born to be. I hate that.

I've had hundreds of conversations about fear and courage. It becomes a central topic whenever we aim to renew ourselves. Repeatedly, I turned to one of my favorite quotes on the topic. It comes from Cus D'Amato, one of the greatest boxing trainers of all time. He used to train World Heavyweight Champion Mike Tyson. If anyone knows about fear, it's Cus. Here's what he said about fear:

"I tell my kids, what is the difference between a hero and a coward? What is the difference between being yellow and being brave? No difference. Only what you do. They both feel the same. They both fear dying and getting hurt. The man who is yellow refuses to face up to what he's got to face. The hero is more disciplined and he fights those feelings off and he does what he has to do. But they both feel the same, the hero and the coward. People who watch you judge you on what you do, not how you feel."
— Cus D'Amato, American Boxing Manager and Trainer

The key is not being immune to fear. Everyone feels it. The key is to keep moving and keep going despite the fear. What you feel is irrelevant. What you do makes all the difference.

Since I founded my business, I have been meeting fear on Main Street at high noon every day. I don't know what tomorrow will bring. I don't know what the next quarter of the year will look like. And I don't have a backup plan.

But I show up every day. I put one foot in front of the other. I keep moving forward. And I keep winning. I keep living the life I want and traveling the career path I created in my head. If it all ended tomorrow, I would die proud, having been brave enough to try. Brave enough to leave a predictable path for the potential of a greater reward on many levels. The fear just makes the victories sweeter.

Create big plans and goals for yourself. You should want to become a better you. And perhaps your most important goal is to step towards the fear and fight through it.

LAST BITE

We all feel fear. It is hardwired into us. But fear is just a yellow traffic light. You get to choose whether you treat it like a red light or a green light.

CHAPTER 73

IF YOU ARE trying to become smarter, stronger, and more capable every day, you need to keep your ears open for good advice. The problem is that not all advice is good. And most certainly, not all advice is right for you. If you're trying to become a better entrepreneur, employee, parent, student, athlete, or friend, how do you know when to listen to advice? And how do you know when to *leave it to Beaver?*

I read a great quote from Britnie Turner, Founder and CEO of Aerial Development Group in Nashville. I don't know Britnie, but I know she is a successful entrepreneur. I know that a percentage of the profits from each home her organization sells directly supports orphans and local nonprofits. (And I know that spellcheck desperately wants to change her name to Britain.)

"Only listen to people you want to be like, and only in that area of their life."
— Britnie Turner, via @britnieturner on Instagram

Her advice is excellent. The point is clear. Only take advice from people who are already doing what you want to be doing. Learn the tips and tricks of the people who behave the way you want to behave. Don't listen to every voice in the wind. Carefully curate the advice you accept.

I love the second part of the message as much as the first. The qualifier ". . .only in that area of their life" is important. I believe in "sliver mentors," role models who can teach you how to do specific things very well. It can be anything from how to make a great introduction, give kind feedback, respond to email, or show your significant other that you are thinking about them during a busy day.

We all have to develop our advice filters. Doing so starts by knowing what we want our fully formed selves to be like. Study, listen, and learn from the people who are already doing what you want to do. But don't let them overstep their areas of influence. Uncle Vern might be great at teaching you how to fish, but that doesn't mean you want to dance, dress, or do business the way he does. So remember to keep the Q-tips handy. That way, when people who don't already align with your ideals offer advice, it can quickly go in one ear and right out the other.

LAST BITE

Know what you want to become, then seek role models to teach you how to do specific things well. Study, listen, and learn from them.

CHAPTER 74

I HAVE HAD the chance to work with Blake Pieroni, who won a gold medal for swimming at the 2016 Olympics in Rio as part of the 4×100 freestyle relay and two gold medals at the 2020 Olympics in Tokyo as part of the 4×100 freestyle relay and the 4×100 medley relay. While filming with Blake, I asked the Indiana native and Indiana University graduate about the major breakthroughs in his career. I was surprised to hear this Olympic gold medalist say he really hasn't had any.

Blake said his progress has been steady and incremental. Day after day, he continues to invest time in his training and preparation. As a result, he has slowly gotten faster. (That is a ridiculous thing to write.) Yet, it's a proven, oxymoronic formula for success.

Blake's career is a testament to the power of slow and steady progress. It is not showy. Or gimmicky. It's not based on shortcuts or nepotism or your famous mama paying to get you into USC. Instead, it's a get-rich-slow scheme. And if you are willing to put in the work it takes, it is the surest way to keep reaching beyond your previous best.

When I launched The Weaponry in 2016, I bootstrapped the business (an Arkansas-sounding way of saying the business was self funded). We did not grow by adding one giant account. We've grown by steadily accumulating great clients and growing our businesses in partnership with those clients.

I was looking at numbers related to company revenue in the spring of 2019 when I noticed something interesting. At just two and a half months into the year, we had already generated more revenue than we did in all of 2016. Yet, we hadn't acquired an Amazonian-sized client. We didn't go Uberish and quadruple our pricing due to heavy rain and an umbrella shortage. Instead, we accumulated seventeen active clients and treated each one like they mattered to our success, because they did.

I also started writing a blog when I launched the agency. My goal was to tell the story of my entrepreneurial journey. I wanted to share my experiences and challenges so that others could benefit from my learnings.

Coincidentally, I noticed an interesting statistic about my blog. By March of 2019, the blog had surpassed the total number of visitors and viewers it had in all of 2016, and my posts had generated 14 times more *likes* than the entire first year. And by *likes,* I mean signs of social appreciation from readers. (Not *likes* written into the body of my posts, because I write like a sixteen-year-old, like, from Likesylvania.)

The business and blog growth are both very rewarding, especially because they are growing too slowly to notice on a daily basis. But when I look at the year-over-year data, the results are clear.

Remember to keep swimming. Keep doing what you know you need to do to get better. Whether it is swimming, writing, growing a business, studying, or any other pursuit. The progress might never be obvious or dramatic. But keep at it anyway. If you do, eventually, you will turn around and notice just how far you have come.

LAST BITE

It is the cumulative progress that matters. Not the speed. Not the attention. Just the results.

CHAPTER 75

Find Your Secret Language And Master It.

MY SON JOHANN has always been musical. He hummed before he could talk. He sang before he got his first haircut. And he memorized lyrics to songs before he started preschool. Thankfully, my wife and I were smart enough to pick up on this talent. We started Johann on piano lessons when he was five years old. He took to it naturally. Before he even outgrew his baby lisp, he was pounding out songs on our piano at home.

A few months after Johann started playing the piano, I was tuning a guitar. My five-year-old budding virtuoso walked past as I was strumming and said, "That sounds like a *G* Dad." I stopped what I was doing, looked at him, and said, "It is a G!"

The question was, how could this five-year-old piano player recognize a G on the guitar? I wondered if he could recognize other notes, so I plucked other strings and asked Johann if he knew what they were. Sure enough, he named them all with ease. E, A, D, G, B, E.

I quickly researched perfect pitch and learned that it is the ability to identify musical notes. People with perfect pitch can typically create the sound of a note perfectly without assistance or reference, and they can dissect the notes in a chord. (In other words, they are freak shows.)

Armed with this new information, I went to our piano and asked Johann if he could make the sound of middle C. He quickly produced a hum. I hit the middle C key on the piano and had a perfect match. Weird. Then, I tried what seemed really far-fetched. I asked him to face away from the piano. I then played two notes at the same time and asked him what notes they were. He nailed them both. I played two other notes. He nailed those, too. Then I played a three-note chord, and he named all three.

It was then that I realized that Johann spoke a language that I didn't speak, and very few people do. In fact, only about 1 in 10,000 people have perfect pitch. Typically, people who develop PP (#snicker) have musical training before the age of six. Unfortunately, we lose our ability to develop perfect pitch after the age of nine.

Recognizing his unique musical abilities and interest, we have leaned into his natural skills and talents. He is now 14 years old and plays the piano, violin, and saxophone. He performs in state piano competitions. And he can do things with a harmonica that make me think he could follow in the lip-steps of Willie Nelson, Bob Dylan, or John Popper.

We all understand a secret language that most others don't. Music is just one example. For others, it may be finance, sales, or compassion. For others still, it may be baking, sports, mechanical interactions, or makeup. We all have at least one rare language that we are born with a natural ability to speak and understand.

The key is for you to identify what that language is and lean into it *hard*. Become fluent. Add value to the world through your mastery of that language. And it is likely to bring you great happiness and wealth.

While Johann speaks the elegant and beautiful language of music, God gave me the ability to make wordplay out of anything. (It feels more *carny* than Carnegie Hall. But hey, I'll take what I can get).

I knew as soon as I learned to read that I had the innate ability to create headlines. I loved reading them in newspapers and magazines. I loved the way they quickly summarized stories with a clever twist. I always thought that being a *headline writer* would be the perfect job for me, that and *chocolate milk drinker.*

When I took my first advertising class, I was hooked. I got straight A's in everything advertising-related. I enjoyed the strategy and the creativity of it immensely. My college professor, Roger Rathke recognized my abilities and connected me with Paul Counsell, the CEO of Cramer Krasselt, one of the greatest ad agencies in America. Paul hired me and gave me my start as a writer.

I have spent my career speaking my secret language. I have enjoyed it tremendously. Clients and co-workers value my thinking. As a result, fun and interesting opportunities keep coming my way.

You can do the same thing with your secret language. Pay close attention to that thing that comes easily to you. Discover it. Develop it. And do amazing things with it. It doesn't matter if you are young or old. Tap into your secret language, and you will have tapped into your path to the greatest happiness, value, and financial success.

LAST BITE

You have a secret language that enables you to perform at a very high level. A level that most people have no chance of ever achieving. Specialize in your secret language and play to your strengths. It makes you feel smart and strong. It makes you feel comfortable. It makes you valuable to others. And when you provide great value to others, it translates to happiness and wealth, two powerful forces we can all understand.

CHAPTER 76

EVEN TWO DECADES after graduation, I have not found a school I would rather have attended than the University of Wisconsin. There is no other town like Madison and no other culture like the university and its work hard, play hard, jump around hard students and alumni.

In college, I double majored in psychology and journalism. I may have also set some sort of school record for most bars and parties attended without drinking alcohol.

In addition to being a student, I was a proud member of the Men's Track & Field team. I threw the discus, the hammer, the 35-pound weight, and the occasional hissy fit.

Every Fall, the track year would kick off with a mandatory team meeting in an auditorium in the McClain Athletic Center.

We had to fill out various forms before we were cleared to participate. It was more business-y than athletic-y. But it signaled the start of the season, and it was the first time the team assembled each school year.

My favorite part of the meeting was when our head coach Ed "Nutty" Nuttycombe addressed the team. When I joined the program, Nutty had already won several Big Ten championships. By the time he retired, he had amassed 26 Big Ten titles. That's more than any other coach in any sport in Big Ten history. I am proud to be part of that history. Our team swept the Big Ten Cross Country, Indoor, and Outdoor track titles during my junior and senior years.

Nutty's Accolades:

- 26 Big Ten Titles
- 2007 NCAA Indoor National Team Championship
- 165 Big Ten Individual Champions
- 11 NCAA Individual Champions
- 6 Olympians

There was one part of this annual meeting I will never forget. Nutty always made a strong point about how he expected us to set our priorities. He said:

"Gentlemen, as a member of this team, always remember that academics come first. You are a student at the University of Wisconsin first. Track and Field comes second. Let me be absolutely clear about that. But if you want to be on this team,

track better be so close behind your school work that you can barely tell the difference. Academics are priority 1. Track and Field is priority 1A."

— Ed Nuttycombe

I remember being surprised the first time I heard this speech. I thought he was going to say academics were always the priority and that athletics came second. But that's not The Nutty Way. In his world, if you can't fully dedicate yourself to both high academic and athletic achievement, then you don't belong on his team. That was a badass statement. And we all felt badass for living up to his standards.

A few years ago, Nutty was inducted into the University of Wisconsin Athletic Hall of Fame. And with great reason. But I would also induct Nutty into the Prioritizing Hall of Fame for how he pushed us to achieve great things in multiple areas of our lives. My teammates were impressive on the track, in the field, and in the classroom. And I am just as proud of the successes they have today in their careers and as husbands and fathers.

I carry on Nutty's dual commitment today to my family and my work. I don't think about balancing the two. I think about prioritizing them both. I must succeed at both. That's what Nutty taught me. And just look at his track record. #PunIntended

LAST BITE

There is no way around it. There are no shortcuts to take. There are no excuses.

CHAPTER 77

I DON'T BELIEVE in work-life balance. It implies that our work and our lives are two separate entities. They are not. Those hours you spend at work each day comprise a gigantic chunk of your life. If you are not happy at work, you are not only wasting your career, you are wasting your life. Those are just the facts.

The notion of a work-life balance implies a teeter-totter life construct. It requires our work to sit on one side of the fulcrum and our lives to sit on the other. It implies that the two sides are separate but equal and balanced.

Other than in fairy tales, outer space, and 1960's TV programs, you are never going to find the two of equal weight. And that is why I am a registered *Work-Life Balance Atheist*. (I still believe in God, Jesus, and Sampson.)

Instead of work-life balance, I believe in work-life integration. We need to construct our lives as a system where all the parts work together to provide a natural flow. When our personal lives need to step forward and take the lead, they naturally do, even during the workday. When work needs us to attend to it, even if we are at home or on vacation, we can naturally allow that to happen, too.

As a business owner, my life and my work are inextricably linked. You are no different. The sooner you and your employer (or employees) accept that, the sooner you can create a happier, more satisfied coexistence between the two.

This work-life integration is why my family relocated our home base from Atlanta to Milwaukee in the fall of 2016. There's a story behind this 800 mile move north.

In the summer of 2015, I began serious plans to start my advertising agency. It was an exciting time in my career as visions and logistics danced through my head. At the same time, a major storm was brewing in my personal life.

On an ordinary August evening in Wausau, Wisconsin, my mother-in-law, Cynthia Zabel, coughed up blood. Fortunately, she called her doctor and saw him the next day. He ordered an MRI, which revealed a small spot on her lung. He decided to do a biopsy to investigate. The biopsy revealed a benign tumor that the doctors decided to remove.

My wife Dawn flew home to Wausau, from Atlanta, to be with her mom during her surgery. Everything was calm and routine until the doctor emerged from the operating room following the operation. He pulled Dawn aside and told her the news, "Well, that didn't go as planned. We didn't see the tumor we were expecting to see. Instead, one of your mother's lungs was completely encased in a tumor. I had two options. I could leave everything exactly as it was and we would take our chances, or I could remove the entire lung. And that is what I did."

So Dawn's mom, at 78-years old, suddenly had only one lung. And, as the new biopsy would reveal, she was dealing with two forms of non-smoking-related lung cancer. She quickly prepared for aggressive chemotherapy and radiation that would give her every chance of survival.

Our tribe quickly rallied around us, including our close friend and Atlanta neighbor, Dr. Crain Garrot, an oncologist. He became our cancer translator and counselor throughout the process. My uncle, Allan Sprau, used his connections to get us an immediate appointment with a specialist at the Mayo Clinic. And Cynthia had her own tribe. With good reason, she felt she was in good hands with her local doctors because she had battled cancer with the same team before and won. By this time, she was a 14-year breast cancer survivor. She trusted her doctors to help her navigate through the new and more daunting challenge.

Cynthia's cancer diagnosis had a significant impact on our family's life plans. Since Dawn and I were planning to start a business, we believed we could locate it anywhere. With the cancer battle ramping up, and my parents reaching retirement age, it was time to make proximity to our parents a priority.

We considered relocating to these four great cities: Chicago, Milwaukee, Madison, or Minneapolis. After visiting each of them and doing a thorough evaluation, we decided on Milwaukee. One year after Cynthia first coughed up blood, we moved into a nice home on a one acre lot, with a pond, in Milwaukee's northern suburb of Mequon. It offered excellent schools and a good quality of life for our family of five. This great city on a great lake put us right between Cynthia in Wausau, Wisconsin, and my parents in Lafayette, Indiana.

We launched The Weaponry in Atlanta and moved it to Milwaukee without missing a beat. And just like that, Atlanta had paid back Milwaukee for taking the Braves in 1966.

Today my mother-in-law is 84 years old and doing great. But even better, we live close enough to drive to see her, even for just a few hours, and then drive home again. It is exactly what we envisioned when we decided to integrate our work and personal needs to be closer to our parents during this chapter of our lives and theirs.

We didn't try to strike a balance between work and life. As a result, Dawn and I have been able to regularly spend quality time with both of our parents here in Wisconsin. And that makes me feel like I am winning at life.

LAST BITE

Integrate your career and life plans into one beautiful, fully functioning design. Don't force the two to fight against each other. And don't settle for less.

CHAPTER 78

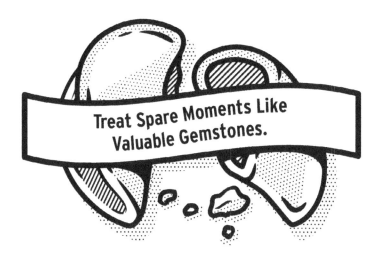

I LOVE THE mulligan that every new year brings. If you are like most people, you resolve to have the "best year yet!" every New Year's Day or birthday. According to my quick and dirty research, these are four basic ways to improve your life:

1. You can start something good.
2. You can quit something bad.
3. You can make a habit of something positive.
4. You can generally just stop being lame.

I have one goal that will help make this year the best year in my career and personal life. Simply stated, I want to make the most of my remnant time.

We all have a slew of things we have to do. They include standard work and home obligations. But like that oft-forgotten 'r' in February, we also have time in the middle of every day that we overlook. But at the start of the new year, I envision all that I can do with my remnant time in the next twelve months.

I am considering adding this quote to the back of my next round of business cards:

"Guard well your spare moments. They are like uncut diamonds. Discard them and their value will never be known. Improve them and they will become the brightest gems in a useful life."
— Ralph Waldo Emerson

Apparently, Ralph Waldo was into bling.

Today, consider what you can do with the time hidden between your must-dos. Instead of killing time with digital thumb-twiddling or catching Zs, spin that time-straw into gold.

I challenge you to use your remnant time to do the things the perfect version of you would do. Read something, write something, create something, solve something, learn something, experience something, accomplish something, improve something, or give something. Or maybe buy a thesaurus and find other words to use instead of "something."

Like compound interest, even little moments add up over the course of a year. Two months ago, I began picking up my daughter's guitar each night and practicing for just a few minutes. And while I'm no Eddie Van Halen, a little invested time each night enables me to play most Christmas songs well enough to keep from getting booed off stage at a nursing home.

I started my business in my spare time. I looked for little moments at night, on the weekends, or over my lunch hour to research, plan and create the business. And like Andy Dufresne, by using my remnant time wisely, I was able to create a path to the place I always wanted to be. Except, unlike Andy, I didn't have to crawl through an active sewer pipe. And chances are, neither will you.

Make the most of each year by making the most of your spare time. Use it to make magic in your career. Strengthen your connections to family and friends. Start that business you always wanted to start. Read more. Finally do those things you have always wanted to do.

LAST BITE

Use your spare moments to have more fun, learn something new, and accomplish more than ever. Start today. You have 1,440 minutes every day.

CHAPTER 79

IN THE SPRING of 2020, I spent three days speaking to smart people at a giant trade show in Las Vegas. Just as the World Health Organization was recommending that we should barricade ourselves in our closets to avoid the COVID-19 virus, I decided to hang out with 100,000 trade show attendees in Sin City. I like to roll the dice.

I was at CONEXPO, a mammoth construction industry show. It is like the construction industry's Super Bowl. Only without the extravagant halftime show. Or football. In any case, it is the largest trade show in the history of my personal trade show experience.

My agency works with CONEXPO. As part of our effort, I was at the show to ask people why they came. One particular attendee had a very simple way of answering that question.

"We have the old way of doing things down. We need to find the new way."
— CONEXPO Attendee

I love this idea. It is easy to master a way of doing things and think that you can simply repeat that process, technique, or approach for the rest of your days. But if you do that, you will stop growing. You will stop improving. You will stop learning. And you will forfeit your competitive advantage to those who continue looking for the 'new' way. The better way. The faster, easier, and more profitable way.

Always be growing. Technology and innovation are continuously improving. We can instantly exchange information and cat videos across the globe. That means that we have unprecedented access to new information and ideas to help improve virtually everything. That includes how we think.

I worked in the advertising industry for 19 years before I started my agency. But from day one, the technology and applications we implemented at The Weaponry were completely different from those I had previously used. We had done our homework and found smarter ways to create our work. And to collaborate with our teammates and partners.

As the company continues to operate and grow, we continue challenging assumptions. We are open-minded and ready to advance as soon as the advancements are ready for us. You should challenge assumptions and be ready to advance, too.

LAST BITE

Once you have mastered the old way, start looking for the new way. Always be learning, growing, and improving. Embrace change. Put innovation and advancements to work for you. They provide a competitive advantage. And if you don't utilize them, your competition will.

CHAPTER 80

I DON'T LIKE rules. It's not that I don't like order, it is that I am wired to find scenarios where the rules don't work. I love discovering conditions where something other than the rule is better than the rule itself. And I especially love pointing out these exceptions in rule-heavy environments, like schools, libraries, and school libraries.

All the rules that the COVID-19 crisis suspended were interestingly satisfying. They provided evidence that rules are not really rules. They are general agreements we make for now. And when a change in conditions warrants, those general agreements can be unmade.

The COVID-19 crisis introduced an endless parade of rule changes for schools, businesses, the Olympics and more, changing start dates, end dates, and requirements of all sorts. We rethought rules about drug trials, telemedicine, sports, and even rules about rules — all the rethinking made for a really interesting time.

Rules that prohibited employees from working from home went out the window when everyone was told they had to work from home. Rules about how long you could hold onto a library book changed. And church rules now say we can't show up for Sunday morning church service. Where was that rule when I was twelve?

I knew we were getting into new territory when the tax deadlines changed. Paying taxes (one of life's certainties) got pushed off for several months. At the same time, criminals stopped serving time for breaking rules that typically would put them behind bars. And speaking of bars, the crazy rule that you couldn't smoke in a bar was beaten by the crazier rule that you couldn't drink in one either.

The closing of everything and the extreme measures taken to combat the health and economic challenges of COVID-19 illustrate that rules can be changed whenever necessary to serve the greater good. So we must keep in mind that we can regularly and temporarily modify rules to serve the smaller, individual good.

LAST BITE

Remember that rules don't rule—the people who make them do. And people can change the rules at anytime to accommodate unusual conditions. It's a reminder for those of us charged with making and enforcing rules to always have the flexibility to acknowledge the exceptions and respond appropriately, compassionately, and creatively.

CHAPTER 81 (EXTRA COOKIE!)

ENTREPRENEURSHIP IS LIKE joining the *Stress of the Day Club* because entrepreneurship is hard. But motherhood and fatherhood and living in the hood are also hard. That's because life is hard and stressful. No one is immune. And not to spoil the ending, but none of us will make it out alive.

We accumulate stress during regular operating hours every day. If we are not careful, that stress can lead to the accumulation of funky gunk. That gunk prevents us from performing at our best. It turns us into cranky pants. It also prevents us from being able to handle more stress.

Three things help me eliminate the stress gunk in my trunk. Together they form my de-stress recipe. (Or destressipe.)

1. Exercise:

I started lifting weights when I was a freshman in high school, and it changed my life. I tend to have a lot of energy and lifting weights helps me burn off my excess, pent-up, or silly energy. Stress is a form of energy, too. You can use it as a workout supplement to move more weights or endure longer endurance-y things. The key is to work out until you've burned off the stress energy. It's a great way to prevent your mind and body from going all Chernobyl.

2. Sleep:

Sleep is your giant reset button. It is what helps replenish your store of energy, your tolerance for craziness, your focus, your stamina, and your eye boogers. Whenever I get seven hours of sleep at night, I feel like I am unstoppable. I often nap on the weekends too, because it is an investment in a better me. When I don't feel quite right, sleep is my go-to prescription. It is how your body naturally regenerates the best you.

3. Church:

Stress often causes us to lose perspective. Or maybe it is the loss of perspective that causes the stress. Either way, attending church is the best way I know to regain a healthy worldview. I believe there is a greater power than me. And I don't just mean the IRS or Dwayne Johnson. I'm on Team Christian. But I believe that all the major league religions provide great perspective and guidance on how to be a better you and live a better life.

I try to attend church regularly. It helps me refocus, refresh, relax, feel supported, and be forgiven for my mistakes. Stresses, frustrations, and losses accumulate every day. Daily setbacks drain us. So we have to prevent the stress gunk from building up and fouling our systems. The key is to figure out how to reboot, regenerate, and respond positively.

LAST BITE

Exercise, sleep, and church are the back to basics keys that can help you find your balance again when you start to weeble or wobble. Try these proven approaches. They just may make you feel like a better human.

CONCLUSION

ARISTOTLE ONCE SAID, "We are what we repeatedly do." Actually, he probably said that more than once. In fact, he probably made a habit of it. Because it is a really good quote, and it is a powerful idea that helps us alchemize our habits into results.

One of the best habits you can develop is to look back regularly to evaluate which of your habits are helping you and which ones are not. Your habits will help grow your skills and abilities. Habits compound over time and create extreme advantages. You can become a profoundly better version of yourself simply by improving what you repeatedly do. Or by focusing on things to not do.

As we wrap up this book, I want to share the habits that work hardest for me. They may also work for you. At a minimum, I hope they inspire you to discover your own most valuable habits.

Now and then, come back to this list to check in on how things are going. What are you doing well? What could you be doing better?

1. Set an alarm.

I set my alarm every day except Christmas, when I know my kids will wake me up early. It goes off at 6:00 am every weekday and no later than 6:30 am on the weekends. I get up and either write or work out first thing. Setting an alarm helps you get the most out of each day, including weekends, vacation days, and holidays.

2. Work hard.

It pays off. You have probably heard that before. I attribute much of what is working for me to hard work. There just isn't an easy way to accomplish great things without it. Putting in work is like planting seeds for later success. So plant as many seeds as you can each day. Then watch them grow.

3. Read more.

I read a lot of books, magazines, and graffiti. It's the best way to end each year smarter, with many more ideas and way more knowledge than you had at the beginning of the year. Regular disciplined reading can have the same effect as taking college courses. So go back to school on your own education.

4. Exercise regularly.

Exercise is a critical part of my personal program. If I don't burn off some of my energy regularly, it brings out my inner Chris Farley.

Exercising regularly helps with physical health, mental health, injury prevention, and self-image. Develop your own weekly exercise habit and enjoy the way it makes you feel every day.

5. Get your ideal sleep.

I have made it a priority to get more sleep over the past few years. When I do, it helps. Going to bed early is like sleeping in for productive adults. Experiment with your sleep needs. Determine how much you need to feel your best. Then build the rest of your day around that number. You'll be amazed by the widespread impact of this habit.

6. Write down your thoughts.

I started a blog in 2015 and have now shared hundreds of posts. To date, my blog has been read in 130 countries, which is crazy in any language. It has helped me share my entrepreneurial experiences, as well as career and life lessons all over the big blue marble. It helps me stay connected with people. But most importantly, writing helps you discover the "Last Bites" from everything that happens to you. It helps you crystalize and sharpen your thinking. You can write a personal journal, a blog or a book. Set a regular schedule for your writing. It will give you a place to write down all the silly things you want to blurt out in important meetings.

7. Ask for introductions.

I have met some of the most interesting, enjoyable, and influential people I know by simply asking for introductions.

Always be looking for people you want to meet. These are people you can learn from. People who will expand your thinking, inspire you, or become a positive influence on your life. Make the request of a mutual contact if you have one. Or simply introduce yourself if you don't. Be purposeful with this habit and it can have a transformative impact on your life.

8. Talk to students and recent graduates.

It is easy to ignore young people as they are just starting their personal and professional journeys. But don't. Make time for the juniors who are interested in talking to you. Those conversations can lead to mentorship opportunities and employment possibilities. By spending time with young people just starting out you can develop relationships with mutual benefits that last a lifetime.

9. Guest lecture.

I enjoy guest lecturing for both high school and college classes. It gives me an opportunity to share what I know, meet new people, and get exposed to new perspectives and talent. Offer to share your expertise and experience. An hour of your day could have a life-altering impact on someone who needs to hear what you have to say.

10. Take vacations.

Travel is great for your mental health, creativity, world perspective, relationships, and airline status. My family and I travel together regularly. We always come back with new stories, memories, and Christmas ornaments. Take your vacation days. They are vital to your well-being, happiness and growth. Schedule regular vacation times each year. Plan them in advance to make sure they happen. You will always have something to look forward to.

11. Take on projects with short turnaround times.

My team and I have taken on some crazy work with extremely short timelines. While rush projects are never ideal, getting things done that even our clients didn't think could be done builds a lot of credit and camaraderie. It has also taught me that there are two very different ways to spell comradery. Make a habit of taking on your own quick turnaround projects. They are often loaded with opportunities. They can make you a hero to someone who needs your help. And they remind you what you are truly capable of.

12. Get involved.

I volunteer my time, talent and attention regularly. By doing so you add horsepower to machines that may not have an engine of their own. Find causes you care about, that you think will help make the world a better place. Offer to help however you can. Make a positive impact without expecting a return and the universe will reward you for your contribution.

13. Go on dates.

My wife Dawn and I went on a lot of dates pre-COVID-19. We made dinner dates, breakfast dates, lunch dates, movie dates, and weekend-away dates. I wish we could do even more. I really like her. And I really like getting her all to myself. Don't get me wrong. I am not recommending that you date my wife. I just highly recommend making time for regular dates with *your* significant other. It gives you time to make each other your single most important priority. It helps you create new shared experiences, which turn into memories. Dates offer time to communicate. They offer great opportunities to have fun. Life is short. Have fun while you can.

14. Coach.

I have coached my son Magnus's football teams for several years and I volunteer as the throwing coach for my daughter Ava's high school track and field team. Both of them have been extremely rewarding experiences. By coaching you can ensure that kids enjoy a fun and encouraging experience. You get a chance to share what you know. It also enables you to develop positive relationships with other children. Today I regularly hear kids yelling, "Hey Coach!" at school events. It's pretty fun. Although I always turn expecting to see Craig T. Nelson.

15. Make your commutes productive.

I try to make the most of my 30 minute commute to work and home. I pack that time full of audiobooks and podcasts. By doing this you can always arrive smarter than when you left. You can also use your commutes to make phone calls to keep in touch with your people. Or you can offer your commute as a great time to talk to people who want to talk to you. Just imagine how much more you could do with your commute time by putting it to work for you.

16. Smile.

I smile a lot. Smiling is my favorite. People comment on the fact that I smile a lot, a lot. (#NotATypo) I attribute much of the positivity I get from the universe and its inhabitants to the fact that I smile a lot. Make a habit of smiling. Make it your default. It makes you seem approachable, interested and interesting. If you want to put just one thing that works for me to work for you, try smiling more.

A FINAL THOUGHT.

NOW THAT YOU have finished this book, collected the fortunes, and absorbed the ideas, it is your turn. Reflect on what is and isn't working for you. Do more of what is working.

But if you add only one thing, add the smiling. Smiling will never let you down.

ACKNOWLEDGMENTS

I AM INCREDIBLY blessed and thankful to have so many people supporting and encouraging me. Starting with my wife, Dawn. You are an incredible human being. You are my great enabler. And not in a need-for-rehab kind of way. Thanks for helping me live my best life.

Thanks to my parents Robert and Jill Albrecht, who provided a rock-solid foundation. You made me feel as if my personal success was guaranteed. I just needed to make it happen. Thanks for always making me and my sisters feel like the priorities in all of your life decisions, even if we weren't.

Thanks to my children for staying out of my office as I wrote. And for all of the other good things you have brought to my life. Ava, Johann, and Magnus, you have all taught me more than you know. I wanted to make sure you had this collection in case I got thrown in prison during your formative years. Or got a wicked case of laryngitis. Or fell into a sinkhole.

Thanks to my sisters Heather, Alison, and Donielle for being so supportive, fun, and funny. And for that crazy birthday thing we have. Go May!

Thanks to my Aunt Deanie Sprau, who magnetized me towards Madison, Wisconsin, where I went to college. Thanks for all the support and food along the way. You have had a tremendous impact on the course of my life. Sorry about that time I left my couch in your driveway.

Thanks to my team of Weapons at The Weaponry. You are constant reminders of why you should surround yourself with great people. Preferably people with weapons that are pointing away from you.

Thanks to my high school track coach, Jude Dutille, who taught me how to throw the discus, shot, and javelin. At the track banquet at the end of my freshman year in high school, you declared that I would be a state champion my senior year. That helped me establish a process of envisioning, goal setting, and self-improvement that would last the rest of my life. And you were right; I would become a state champion. In two events. Just not in the event you thought. And it first happened my junior year. Because I am impatient.

Thanks to my college throwing coach Mark Napier who taught me that the more you believe in someone, the more they believe in themself. Thanks, Napes and Coach Nutty for enabling me to be part of such a special team. Because some teams can't even afford new uniforms.

Thanks to my college professor Roger Rathke who opened the door to my first job in advertising and for serving as my first advertising role model. Roger had done what I wanted to do. And he was an old guy with a cool job and a really cool car.

Thanks to Paul Counsell for being on the other side of the door that Roger opened and for letting me in. Cramer Krasselt was an excellent launch pad for my career. And it was a great place to stalk my future wife.

Thanks to my Uncle Jerry Sprau for bringing me to Wyoming to snowmobile in 1998. We had no way of knowing it then, but that had a huge impact on the trajectory of my career. It also taught me why you shouldn't try to call coyotes.

Thanks to my childhood friend Dan Richards, CEO of Global Rescue, for becoming The Weaponry's first client and providing so much entrepreneurial guidance and encouragement along the way. You showed me that tough things happen all the time and tough people just keep marching anyway. All of the time we spent in the weight room together taught me that we get to create the future version of us that is way better than the current us. And it gives you a false sense of superiority. Which has come in handy over the past few decades.

Thanks to my friend Troy Allen who has taken on so many new challenges in his career that he has encouraged me to think bigger and to appreciate my hair.

Thanks to all my friends who wrote books before me, which made it seem doable.

Thank you to everyone who has read my blog over the past six years. Your feedback and encouragement made me feel like I might be able to write a book people would like and find valuable.

Thank you, Dennis Giglio and Matt Jauchius, for sending me to India in 2018. That trip set some important things in motion to make me want to write a book to share what I know. It also made me wonder why there is so much advertising for cement in India.

Thanks to the Covid-19 lockdown for providing time to focus on bringing this book to life. And making me a better foosball player.

Thank you, Anne Lamott and John C. Maxwell, for your writings. You showed me that simple events can turn into interesting and valuable stories. You were the ones that made me think I could write a book. I appreciate it.

Thanks to Chris Dawson, who first told me that I had no chance of winning his business. He then went on to create numerous great opportunities for me. In fact, Chris was the first person to encourage me to start my own agency. Sometimes that's all it takes.

Thanks to Mark O'Brien for your tremendous support. Your endorsements have meant a lot to me. And your last-minute presentation surprises have kept me on my toes, like an NFL linebacker.

Thanks to my friend and client Nicole Hallada for showing me how giving without expecting anything can provide infinite positive returns.

Thanks to my Maurader and Badger brothers.

Thanks to my teammates at Cramer Krasselt and Engauge. That sure was fun.

Thanks to my giant Albrecht and Sprau families. You make me feel like I have a huge safety net.

Thanks to my cousin Brooks Albrecht, who started The Weaponry with me. I look forward to our next project. The first one is going pretty well.

Thank you to author Marla McKenna for helping guide, inspire, and motivate me to make this book happen. Maybe someday I will get to work with Rick Springfield too.

Thank you to Michael Nicloy for sharing your knowledge about the publishing process. You made me feel like it wouldn't be that hard.

Thanks to my co-hometowns of Norwich, Vermont and Hanover, New Hampshire. It's complicated.

Thanks to Rachelle Kuramoto for being such a great editor. I appreciate your guidance and encouragement throughout this process. You make me think the book is good. Even though I know it's your job.

DMF, your PMing was AOK. TY.

Thanks too Jaye Liptak fir pruf reeding the bewk sew goodly.

Thanks to Jeff Hilimire for repeatedly suggesting that I should write a book. For helping me make it happen. For all the other support and encouragement you have provided through my entrepreneurial journey. For being a constant friend. And for pushing yourself and encouraging others to do the same.

Thank you, God. You were there from the beginning.

ABOUT ADAM ALBRECHT

ADAM ALBRECHT IS the Founder and CEO of the advertising and ideas agency The Weaponry. The agency's broad portfolio of clients ranges from legendary international brands to innovative startups. Prior to The Weaponry, he worked at renowned advertising agencies Cramer Krasselt, Engauge Marketing, and Moxie in roles ranging from copywriter to Chief Creative Officer.

Adam has worked on iconic brands including Reddi-Wip, Nike, Coca-Cola, Dasani, Nationwide Insurance, Wells Fargo, UPS, Hertz, Safelite, Mizuno, Bob Evans, Chick-fil-A, GNC, Universal Studios, AMC Theatres, Volvo, Prevost, SeaDoo, Ski-Doo, and Can-Am.

Adam earned a double major in psychology and journalism from the University of Wisconsin. He also captained the Badgers'

Big Ten Conference Champion track and field team, becoming the number one hammer thrower and number four discus thrower in school history.

In high school, Adam was a two-time New England track and field champion in the discus. His senior year, he set a New Hampshire state record just eight months after undergoing ACL reconstruction surgery.

Today, Adam lives in Milwaukee with his wife Dawn and children Ava, Johann, and Magnus. He enjoys all things outdoors and adventurous. During his free time, he coaches youth football and high school track and field.

You can follow Adam at adamalbrecht.blog where he shares ideas on self-improvement, creativity, and entrepreneurship.

Made in United States
Orlando, FL
07 January 2023